Production
For Print

Mark Gatter

Laurence King Publishing

LAURENCE KING

First published as *Getting it Right in Print* in Great Britain in
2004 by Laurence King Publishing Ltd
This revised and expanded edition published in 2010 by
Laurence King Publishing Ltd
361–373 City Road
London EC1V 1LR
United Kingdom
Tel: + 44 20 7841 6900
Fax: + 44 20 7841 6910
e-mail: enquiries@laurenceking.com
www.laurenceking.com

A catalogue record for this book is available
from the British Library.

ISBN: 978-1-85669-699-9

Design: Studio Ten and a Half
Typeface: Helvetica
Senior Editor: Clare Double
Editorial Director: Jo Lightfoot

Printed in China.
The paper used for this book is from sustainable forests.

Related study material is available on the Laurence King
website at www.laurenceking.com

Contents

Preface

For the past twenty-five years, I have worked extensively in the commercial printing industry and also as a graphic designer, both in the US and in England. I am constantly running into other graphic designers who have a three-year degree course or similarly extensive training behind them, or who have even been working in the industry for years, but who nevertheless have little or no idea about the actual requirements of the printing process. As a result, every time they send a job to their printers, they experience nail-biting anxiety because they don't know exactly how it is going to turn out.

The grey areas that cause this anxiety include dot gain, image calibration, trapping, the use of CMYK vs. RGB, and generating error-free PDF documents for the printer.

This book explains all of these misunderstood areas, and more, in such a way as to provide an overview of the entire process, from error-free digital creation right through to commercial printing. It includes detailed instructions that will enable anyone, even complete beginners, to do the necessary work for themselves before the job is sent to the print shop.

I currently hold the ACE (Adobe Certified Expert) qualification in Photoshop, Illustrator, InDesign, Dreamweaver and Flash, and, as well as writing books on this subject matter, I teach intensive one- and two-day training courses, covering skill levels from complete beginner to advanced, in all those applications as well as in QuarkXPress and CorelDRAW.

I also teach one- and two-day Digital Repro and Pre-press courses specifically aimed at graphic designers, and offer private consultation and troubleshooting on questions relating to graphics, printing and print production.

If you would like to know more, please visit my website (www.markgatter.co.uk) or email me (mark@markgatter.co.uk).

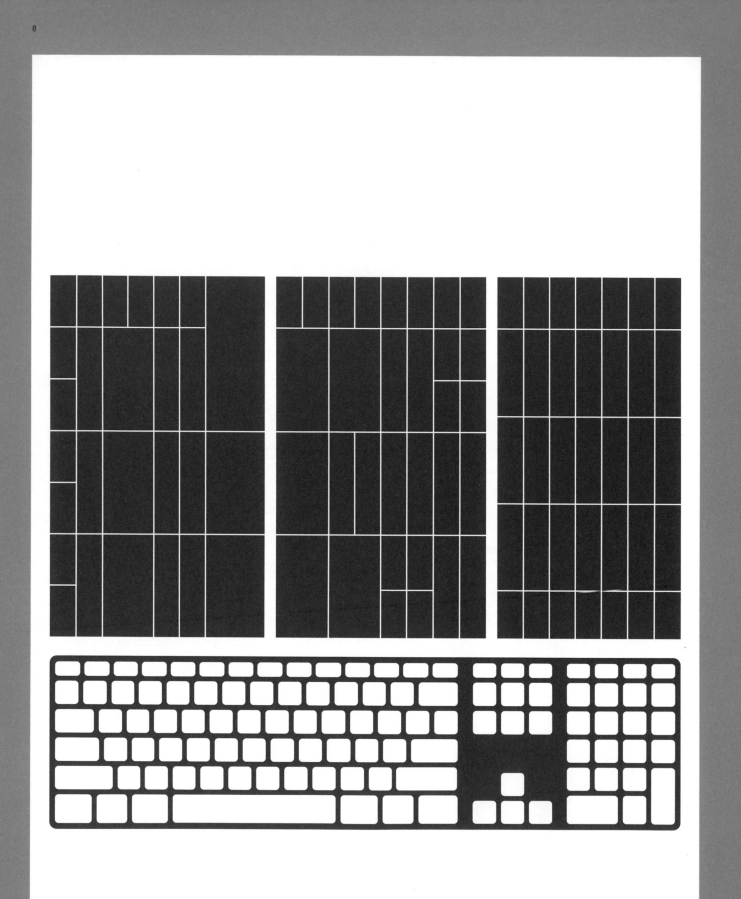

The Evolution of an Industry

1

Printing has been with us for a very long time. We can look back on the evolution of a process which hardly changed at all for several centuries, but which in the last hundred years has been transformed beyond belief. Photography replaced woodcuts; offset litho replaced letterpress; computer graphics replaced metal type, manual artwork assembly *and* the printer's darkroom; and now the internet carries more and more of the information which used to be available only in print. Whether a browser window will eventually replace the printed page remains to be seen, but, for the time being at least, we still need to know how to print things, properly.

Unfortunately, developing technology has always meant that the expert knowledge of the previous methods gradually becomes relegated to specialists, museums and history books, and this is as true of the printing industry as it is of anything else. Sometimes it doesn't really matter, but sometimes we run so fast towards the new approach that, along the way, useful information is discarded along with useless, and we find that we no longer know how to get the result we want.

So here is a short introduction to printing. I have always found that background information is useful because it provides an overview which tells me where I stand, and gives me a foundation on which I can build. I hope it will prove to be the same for you.

Opposite (Above): Layouts of type cases – divided wooden drawers, each compartment holding metal-block characters of a single font in a specific point size.
(Below): A computer keyboard layout: every character you want, in all the available fonts, any time you want it.

The Changing Face of Graphic Design

For many years, the printing industry has been divided into two separate areas of expertise. There are those who run the presses and take care of 'finishing'; i.e. cutting, folding, binding and so on. Other people supply the jobs to be printed: the graphic designers. Since the early 1980s, the work of graphic designers has evolved from the mechanical assembly of the basic layout, into which the printer's photographic department placed the relevant images, to the production of digital files that contain absolutely everything needed for the job.

Digitization has been a major development. Yet, while the methods used to produce digital files continue to evolve at high speed, as each successive version of the various software applications is released, the designer and the printer have generally remained within their own traditionally defined areas of expertise. As a result, many of the physical requirements of the printing process are not understood by the very people who need to understand them most of all – the graphic designers.

In the early days of digital production, graphic designers often went through a period of intense anxiety while they waited to see how their work actually looked in print. Colours might have changed, pictures might look miserable compared to how they appeared on screen, and previously unseen mistakes might suddenly make themselves known.

Rather than improving over time, these problems took a serious turn for the worse in the early 2000s. Printers started to request that jobs were submitted to them as a **PDF (portable document format)** file rather than in the 'native' software in which they were created. While this has made life easier for printers, PDF files are hard – sometimes impossible – to edit. Printers often don't notice unwitting errors, as the nature of PDF files means that these errors are much harder to see in the first place, leaving responsibility for them squarely on the shoulders of the unfortunate designer.

Precise image **calibration, dot gain, RGB** vs. **CMYK**, screen clash and **trapping** are some of the grey areas encountered by graphic designers in digital pre-press. These seemingly complex processes are actually easy to deal with, but they are often not understood, and can lead to problems on the press that are expensive and time-consuming to fix.

Graphic designers who can understand and manage these areas with confidence will save time and money on everything they do. In addition, they will no longer find themselves waking up in a panic at 3 a.m., mentally going over their production process searching for possible errors.

How it All Started

The printing industry has evolved over many centuries, although for hundreds of years the printing process hardly changed. During the past fifty years, however, its acceleration has been phenomenal.

Originally, the complete image of a page was carved onto a piece of wood (fig. **1.1**). This is still done in some parts of the world today. The remaining surface area – the letters – were inked and the cut-out areas were not. When a sheet of paper (or parchment, or vellum) was pressed down onto the wood block and then peeled away carefully, the ink transferred onto the paper and an image was produced. Two tricky things regarding this method were: 1) what happened if there was a typo (typographical error), and 2) typos were more likely to occur because the page had to be carved as a reversed image of what was actually wanted, which is much harder to create accurately.

The invention of moveable type on metal blocks was therefore a huge leap forward. Typos could be fixed quickly and easily and, once the job was finished, it could all be taken apart and used again for the next job. As well as type characters, decorative elements could be created (fig. **1.2**).

Moveable type was first developed in China in 1041 using clay characters. In 1440 Johannes Gutenberg produced the first moveable metal type press in Europe, culminating in the production of the famous Gutenberg Bible in 1455.

Illustrations were combined with type for the first time when Albrecht Pfister printed *Edelstein*, which featured a number of woodcuts, in 1461. Fifteen years later, in 1476, William Caxton started printing in England – using typefaces that were intended to look like monks' handwriting – and by the end of that century printing was taking place in 250 European cities. However, early in the seventeenth century the potential power of the printed word brought strong opposition from both Parliament and the Church. In 1637 an act was passed limiting by decree the number of printers in England. Then, in 1644, the Licensing Act required all printed material to be approved by an official censor. With penalties that included fines, imprisonment, confiscation of equipment and even death, this attempt to preserve the existing power structure was successful. As a result, by the end of the century there were only twenty master printers in England, eighteen in London. Given this kind of obstacle-ridden start, it is amazing that printing survived. No wonder 'freedom of speech' and 'freedom of the press' are taken so seriously today.

1.1 (Left) Printing blocks such as these, in which an entire page is carved into a single piece of wood, are still used in Nepal, Bhutan and Tibet.

1.2 (Below) The use of moveable type, where individual letters were created as separate, reusable metal blocks, meant that printing was suddenly easier, more accurate and much faster than before.

From Letterpress to Litho

For centuries, the only kind of commercial printing available was **letterpress** (fig. **1.3**), a process in which a matrix of assembled metal type characters was first inked and then pressed against a sheet of paper, thus transferring the image. Then, in the early 1830s, photography was invented. This paved the way for all kinds of changes, including new methods for creating the images used in letterpress printing and, somewhat later, in **offset litho** (fig. **1.4**). It took about sixty years for offset litho, first used in the early twentieth century, to steal the bulk of the printing market away from letterpress – a market that was still being fought over into the early 1960s. Even in the late 1970s it was not uncommon to find a letterpress printer working in the corner of what was otherwise an offset-litho shop.

How did this revolution take place? Initially it was through the production of images rather than type. Printers wanted to get away from purely illustrative woodcuts and engravings in favour of realism. But, as with woodcuts and engravings, the problem was how to create all those shades of grey when using just one colour of ink: black. They already knew that this could be achieved by relying on an optical illusion. Small, thin lines in a woodcut image, when printed, looked like a light grey, whereas thicker lines looked darker. Finally, in 1890, after several years of experimentation, an American named Frederick Ives came up with a method that allowed the whole process to become photographic. He engraved a grid of fine horizontal and vertical lines on a sheet of glass. The image was projected through the glass onto the emulsion-coated side of a sheet of unexposed **film**. Since the image could not pass through the engraved lines it instead bounced between them, so what reached the film was not a continuous-tone image (i.e. all the shades of grey between black and white) but spots of light of varying sizes. The result was called a **halftone**. A dark area on the original image would eventually produce a large dot of black ink, whereas a light part would produce a small dot (fig. **1.5**). Before the image made it all the way to the paper, however, there were several other stages to the process.

Initially, film images were used to make exposures onto **plates** of zinc or copper that were coated with a light-sensitive emulsion. These were then etched and mounted onto blocks of hardwood – usually oak or mahogany – for use in letterpress printing in exactly the same way that woodcuts and engravings had been. The surface of the block – the image – would get inked, but the background, having been etched away, would not.

Creating a halftone image on either a letterpress block or an offset-litho plate depends on much the same process. Turn to fig. 1.5. Light reflected from the original image (A) travels through a screen (B) and produces halftone dots of varying sizes on a sheet of film (C). This example shows negative film, which has clear dots on a black background. Using positive film would instead give a black dot on a clear background. While film is nowadays much less common, both positive and negative plate processes are found throughout the printing industry. The image on the film is transferred to the plate (D) through making a 'contact' exposure during which the two elements are held firmly together.

In order to make halftone dots clearer and more consistent, the printing industry had to figure out a new kind of film. The emulsion it used was not required to create shades of grey, because that would produce fuzzy-edged dots – and dots in a halftone need to be crisp and clear. If the edges were fuzzy, nobody could say how big the resulting dot was going to be. That is why printing materials such as film and plates work in a sort of binary fashion – on or off. Either there is a clear dot on the film, or there is not; either there is a resulting ink-holding dot on the plate, or there is not; either there is a resulting dot printed on the paper, or there is not. There are, literally, no grey areas. This is because in order to produce a shade of grey, it is necessary to use either grey ink or the white of the paper showing through between all the black dots and thus creating an illusion of grey when seen from a distance. It is all the art of illusion. Fortunately, graphic designers only need to be convincing, and that is a very important thing to remember. On a printed image, if you are close enough to see the dots, you (almost completely) stop seeing the image – and the illusion is therefore not convincing (fig. **1.6**). However, when you cannot see the dots any more (either because they are too small or too far away) you can only see the (quite convincing) image. Pure illusion. Our job is to maintain the illusion as far as possible. (Incidentally, litho film is also completely insensitive to red light, which means that a darkroom technician can run around in the darkroom while there is film lying about, without bumping into everything.)

1.3 Letterpress printing machines of various types were the main printing method from the time of Gutenberg until the emergence of offset litho in the early 1900s.

1.4 (Below) An offset-litho press. This one, at Epic Print in Dorchester, uses a computer to plate (CTP) workflow.

1.5 (Bottom Left) Generating a halftone from a continuous-tone image.

1.6 (Bottom Right) On the left, we see the dots more than the image. On the right, we see the image more than the dots.

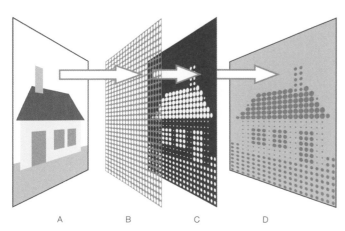

A   B   C   D

Advances in Typesetting

Despite this great leap forward in the production of photographic images, offset litho, while gaining in popularity, had to continue to wait in the wings until the second half of the twentieth century, when new technology was developed for the production of type. The individual metal and wood letters of letterpress were quite quickly pushed to the side by the much faster and cleaner IBM Selectric (the 'golfball' print head typewriter), rub-down type from Letraset (and others), and early **photo-typesetting** machines.

Photo-typesetting was invented in 1949, but did not really become established until the 1960s. These were darkroom-operated mechanical devices that projected the image of the letters, one at a time, onto a strip of photographic paper. Letterspacing was manually controlled until the advent of automatic spacing in systems such as the Monotype Studio Lettering Machine (invented by my father in the early 1970s), a typesetter that was also versatile enough to be able to set type ranging in height from 3mm (⅛in) to 128mm (5in). The prototype of this wonderful device and the several improved versions of later years were built in our garden shed in London.

Computers finally became involved as several manufacturers developed typesetting hybrids that were partly digital and partly mechanical. Type was set using a computer keyboard and a single-colour **CRT (cathode ray tube)** screen and coded in the same kind of way as **HTML (hypertext markup language)**. If you wanted the next line of type to be bold, you had to first type the code that said 'be bold', then the line of text, and then the code that said 'stop being bold'. **Linotype** and **Compugraphic** machines contained a wheel on which four strips of film were clamped, each carrying the entire character set of a particular font – which does not mean, for example, the entire Helvetica family; Helvetica Bold is a font, Helvetica Bold Italic is another. The wheel turned at high speed, and as the appropriate letter passed in front of a strobe light, the light fired. The beam passed through the letter, then through one of five lenses mounted on a rotating turret, then through a prism that projected it up onto a roll of photographic paper. At the end of the job, the paper would be advanced into a light-fast container so that it could be removed and transferred to a film processor. The result was a **galley** of type, sometimes several metres long.

Now, of course, computers have taken over these processes completely – not only for the production of type, but in the creation and editing of images, too. But that is not to say that the printer's darkroom is a thing of the past. As mentioned already, things change slowly in printing. Cutting-edge developments of today might still take several decades to become widespread enough for us to take them for granted. Despite the prevalence today of **computer to plate (CTP)** printing, there are still many print shops all over the world that use their darkrooms on a daily basis. So, film is still very much with us. It is also interesting to note how, in only the last few years, we have gone from a situation in which 'whoever has the most fonts, wins' to 'whoever has the most fonts... simply has the most fonts.' In the days of the Linotype and Compugraphic photo-typesetters, a single font film strip cost around £100 ($165). Having an extensive font library back then was a very serious matter. Now, however, there are websites from which anyone can download fonts for free. However, beware the 'zillion fonts for a buck' collections; these can contain not only fonts of very poor quality, but some that may wreck your whole system.

The Font Wars

Early computer fonts were **bitmapped**, i.e. the letters displayed at a single, fixed resolution. This meant that a separate font file was required for every different type size needed in a job. **PostScript** Type 1 fonts, developed by Adobe, were based on **vector** outlines for each character. As vectors are not resolution-dependent, the lettering in a single font could be scaled to whatever sizes were required. PostScript fonts are made up of two files: one to produce a screen image (the printer font metrics, or pfm file) and the other (the printer font binary, or pfb file) to send the vector outline information to the printer. A huge boost for this format came in 1985 when Apple adopted Adobe's PostScript page description language (PDL) for the Apple LaserWriter printer. So, first we can see Apple and Adobe benefiting from helping each other out: Adobe by coming up with the PostScript format in the first place, and Apple for adopting it, for a suitable fee, as the format of choice.

Unfortunately, PostScript fonts are not cross-platform compatible, so there was still room for improvement. Not surprisingly, bitmapped fonts could not compete against the advantages of scaleability and soon vanished forever.

Apple, Microsoft and (later) IBM all realized that, unless there were new developments in type, Adobe's monopoly would continue forever. Apple was the first of the three to come up with a solution in the form of TrueType. Apple traded its new technology with Microsoft in exchange for the latter's TrueImage PostScript clone technology – despite the fact that it was bug-ridden at the time. So, this second major development saw a partnership between Microsoft and Apple.

TrueType characters are also scaleable vector outlines, but they differ from PostScript in that the fonts are made up of a single digital file. Typographical purists will notice that PostScript characters have a slightly cleaner outline than their TrueType equivalents, but this of course only becomes apparent when they are printed large enough to see each individual outline in great detail. For most work, either will do.

Originally it could sometimes cause problems if a designer used both PostScript and TrueType fonts in the same file. While these early problems were quickly overcome, it is still the case that you should avoid having both TrueType and Type 1 fonts with exactly the same name installed on the same system, whether it is a PC or a Mac.

Multiple Master (MM) font format is an extension of the PostScript Type 1 format. Basically it allows a designer to select two different weights of the same typeface and combine them into a single font at any weight between the two.

The next serious advance in type, OpenType fonts, has seen a partnership between Adobe and Microsoft who, as part of their agreement, have licensed TrueType and PostScript font technologies to each other. OpenType fonts are unique in that the same file will operate on both PC and Mac systems. Previously, sending a job from a PC to a Mac **imagesetter** either required **PostScripting** first, so that the font information was embedded in the PostScript code that the imagesetter understood, or that the font used on the PC was also installed on the Mac. Even then, reflow of text has been a common and serious problem.

As well as being cross-platform compatible, OpenType fonts have the ability to support widely expanded character sets and layout features. They use a single font file for all of the outline, metric and bitmap data, and while all the major graphics applications can make use of OpenType fonts, users of Adobe InDesign can also access OpenType layout features that will automatically substitute alternate **glyphs** such as automatic **ligatures**, small capitals, **swashes** and old-style figures.

Film Technology

Commercial offset lithography, the printing method with which this book is mostly involved, relies on an image that has been photographically generated (an analogue process, i.e. a physical and therefore a 'lossy' transfer) or electrostatically generated (digital, i.e. 'lossless' transfer) on a plate. Plates are typically thin sheets of aluminium coated with a photo-reactive emulsion. When an exposed plate is developed, the image areas tend to attract oil-based inks, whereas the background areas tend to attract water. By keeping a delicate balance between the ink and the water – which is provided by a unit called the damper system – the right stuff sticks to the right areas and what you end up with is something capable of generating a printed image. Although the materials may vary – for example, you can even get paper plates – the basic idea has remained the same. (There is a more detailed discussion of the offset litho process on page 20.)

For an example of how litho film generates a plate, let us assume that we have assembled the art for an entire printed image and taken an accurate photograph of it. This photograph might have been film generated by an imagesetter that got its information from a disk, or it might have been film generated by the paste-up, darkroom and 'film stripping' (highly skilled assembly of film from different sources to make up a complete job) departments in a film-based print shop. In order to make a plate, we have to lay the film, emulsion side down, onto the plate (which is emulsion side up), and expose them both to light in order to transfer the image from one to the other. This is done in a glass-topped vacuum frame that sucks all the air from between the film and plate prior to the exposure to ensure a crisp transfer of image. Specks of dust, or other foreign bodies trapped inside, create intense pinpoints of uneven pressure that show up on the glass as **Newton's Rings** (fig. **1.7**). These are dark, rainbow-coloured concentric circles that show where subsequent problems might occur. Obviously enough, if a foreign object gets caught between the film and the plate in the middle of a halftone, there will be a distortion of the resulting plate image at that point. So the operator scans the whole plate area carefully for any sign of Newton's Rings. If they show up in a potentially dangerous area, the operator turns off the vacuum, waits for the pressure to equalize, then lifts the lid to remove the speck. Sometimes it takes a while to make a good plate. When it finally looks clean, the operator can start the exposure, which is usually done with ultraviolet light. This cooks the surface emulsion and hardens it, so that when the plate is developed, the image is left behind while the background is washed away.

1.7 Newton's Rings.

There are some geographical differences in the process, depending on where in the world you happen to be. In the US, negative-working film and plates are much more common, whereas in Europe and Asia almost everyone uses positive-working materials instead. Either way, it does not make too much difference. Negative plates can (usually) be protected for future use with a thin coating of gum arabic, whereas the image on positive plates will (usually) continue to be affected by light and will not be of much use to anyone shortly after the protective layer of ink has been washed off. Negative plates will (usually) need to be replaced part of the way through very long runs, whereas positive plates can (usually) keep on going well beyond 100,000 impressions. There are, of course, exceptions to these generalizations, but to detail the differences between the most common materials in use worldwide would require a great deal of space, and as it is information that is mostly useful only to a printer trying to match the appropriate materials to a specific job, it is information that is not of much use to a designer. The suitability of that match, however, can be part of the reason why the quote from one print shop might be very different to the quote from another. A good price depends on the availability of the appropriate press and the most cost-effective materials, given the size of the printed piece and the number of copies required.

Film and plate processors are now to be found everywhere, and their use avoids most of the difficulties inherent in manual plate and film developing. Chemicals circulate so that they are maintained at a constant strength, the temperature is held at the optimum level, and working materials are pulled through on rollers ensuring that they are only kept in the various solutions – traditionally a sequence of developer, fixative and wash – for the correct length of time. Plate processors especially are to be found in shops running CTP and **direct imaging (DI)** operations, which do not bother with film at all.

1.8 (Left) An imagesetter producing an offset-litho plate directly from digital information.
1.9 (Below) A digital press, which uses neither plates nor film.

Filmless Technology

Computer to plate (CTP)

CTP technology is now firmly established in the world of print. The obvious advantages of this technology make it clear that the 'traditional' film-based methods will become progressively less common as time goes by. Even so, as printing presses (and related equipment) do not wear out very quickly, the transition to newer methods has always tended to be quite slow.

In a CTP workflow, digital files are used to make plates instead of generating film as a first stage (fig. **1.8**). Because there is no film, image faults caused by foreign objects getting between the film and plate, as well as the expensive and time-wasting revisions they can cause, are a thing of the past. There are also no **registration** problems caused by 'film stretch'. The degradation of dots caused by dot gain (see Chapter 4) is diminished, although not completely, because one of the stages at which the image is physically (rather than digitally) transferred from one medium to another has been removed from the process. Printed images are therefore sharper and registration is better. Environmentally there are benefits, too, because there is no longer a need for the chemicals associated with film processing and manufacture.

Direct imaging (DI)

Direct imaging takes CTP a step further. Not only is film cut out of the process, but the plates themselves are imaged right on the press by an array of lasers. The images thus generated hold ink in just the same way as on conventional offset-litho machines. This means that everything required for the job arrives on-press perfectly positioned – i.e. registered – with no further positioning adjustments required, therefore saving considerable time in getting the job ready to roll. As the main advantage of DI over other methods is this decrease in set-up time, it tends to attract short-run work requiring a fast turnaround.

The best thing about CTP technology is that by removing film from the process, quality is (potentially) increased, and cost and turnaround time are reduced. The best thing about DI technology is that it removes yet another step and sends digital data directly to the press. The next big question, therefore, is whether DI printing will kill off the CTP market in the same way that CTP has almost completely killed off the film market. Again, expect any transition to be slow. CTP is a technology that can be used with conventional presses, and these will continue to have a place on the shop floor for many years to come.

Digital printing

Digital printing presses (fig. **1.9**) are much closer to laser printers than they are to the various offset litho printing methods. Instead of conventional ink, they use either toner or a mix of toner suspended in a liquid vehicle. The image that they print is electrostatically generated on a drum rather than on a removable plate, and with each revolution of the drum the image is generated again. This means two things: first, the cost of generating each page tends not to decrease with volume, and second, each time the drum revolves, the image can be changed. Therefore, with digital printing it is possible to generate just one copy of a multiple-page job such as a book. This makes it a very attractive option for the graphic designer who wishes to produce a convincing high-quality proof for a client.

However, do not expect to find digital printing presses sitting next to conventional offset presses. They are an entirely different animal and require their own unique administrative environment. Because the main advantages of digital printing are, for example, individually targeting all the people on a mass-mailing list, or taking on extremely short runs on extremely tight deadlines, it requires a highly optimized internal workflow developed with specific applications such as mailing and fulfilment, e-commerce and in-house design and photography capabilities. Therefore digital printing presses have a specific customer base that is very different to those who send conventional printing work to conventional printers.

The Offset Litho Process

On a good day, offset litho printing works as follows. Paper is loaded onto a platform at the back end of the press, above which is a series of suckers. These lift the paper, one sheet at a time, and enable the grippers (grabbing pincers mounted on a chain-link drive) to grab it along one edge (called the **gripper edge**) and pull it into the first ink unit, where it is printed with the first colour. As it leaves, it is grabbed again and pulled forwards into the next ink unit, and so on.

Presses vary as to how many ink units they have. Book presses typically have just one ink unit in order to print only black text, and are often very large format to allow many pages to be printed together on a big 'parent' sheet.

Presses used for colour work usually have at least two and preferably four units (for cyan, magenta, yellow and black, the CMYK colours). They may have a fifth and even a sixth unit for a varnish and/or a **spot colour** (i.e. a non-CMYK ink, also called a **special colour**), which is usually a custom Pantone colour mix (see Chapter 10). While four-colour printing can be achieved one colour at a time using a press with a single ink unit, this is far less efficient and more prone to registration problems.

The way an ink unit works is shown in fig. **1.10**. At the top, there is a trough containing ink. Sitting in the trough is a roller that turns slightly every few seconds. Behind this roller is another roller that jumps forwards to touch it, picking up a long bead of ink, then jumps backwards to spin against the other rollers in what is called the inking system. This system is a complex series of rollers designed to bring the ink down onto the plate in a controlled way. Usually only three or four rollers out of the whole array actually touch the plate surface and transfer the ink onto it.

Behind the plate cylinder is another vital set of rollers comprising the dampening system. This is a smaller and simpler unit that uses a similar method to cover the background areas of the plate lightly with a pH-balanced solution, mostly water.

Many people assume that the image is transferred onto the paper by the plate. Not so. The plate is a thin sheet of aluminium (sometimes zinc or another material) and has a hard surface. It would quickly wear out if it had to come into contact with a comparatively abrasive material like paper for very long. Instead, the image is transferred ('offset') onto the blanket cylinder, a roller covered with a canvas-backed sheet of rubber. Hence the term 'offset printing'.

The blanket, being rubber, can press down hard on the paper with no problem. Simultaneously, the impression cylinder presses from underneath. The resulting pressure stops the paper slipping as it moves between the two, creating a sharp image.

After the last unit on the press, the paper hits a stop bar just as the grippers let go of it, and settles onto an ever-increasing pile on another trolley. Typically, **sheet-fed presses** are run at around 3,000 sheets an hour.

Paper is very heavy. It is made mostly from wood pulp, and a stack of it sitting on a pressroom trolley can easily weigh a couple of hundred kilos or more. After the first run through the press, the side facing down is nice clean paper, but the other side, facing up, is fresh, wet ink. So why is it that the clean side of a sheet does not stick to the wet side of the sheet underneath it? (That is also a kind of 'offset', by the way, but in this instance it is called **set-off**.) The answer is quite simple: cornflour. Printers call it 'offset spray' (perhaps 'cornflour' would not sound 'printerly' enough), but it is the same stuff. The idea is that, just as the grippers let go and the sheet starts to fall gently onto the stack, an air blower puffs out a little cloud of offset spray beneath it – just enough to ensure a few particles, and therefore a very small space, is left between each sheet. Offset spray used in this way is too fine to see, but when a stack is dry you can sometimes feel it as a slight roughness on the paper surface.

Since offset spray tends to build up around the end of the press, the printer will occasionally use compressed air to blast it all away – thus creating a whole bunch of potential disasters as accumulated clumps fall from the ceiling and land in the ink system.

1.10 How a single ink unit works on an offset press.

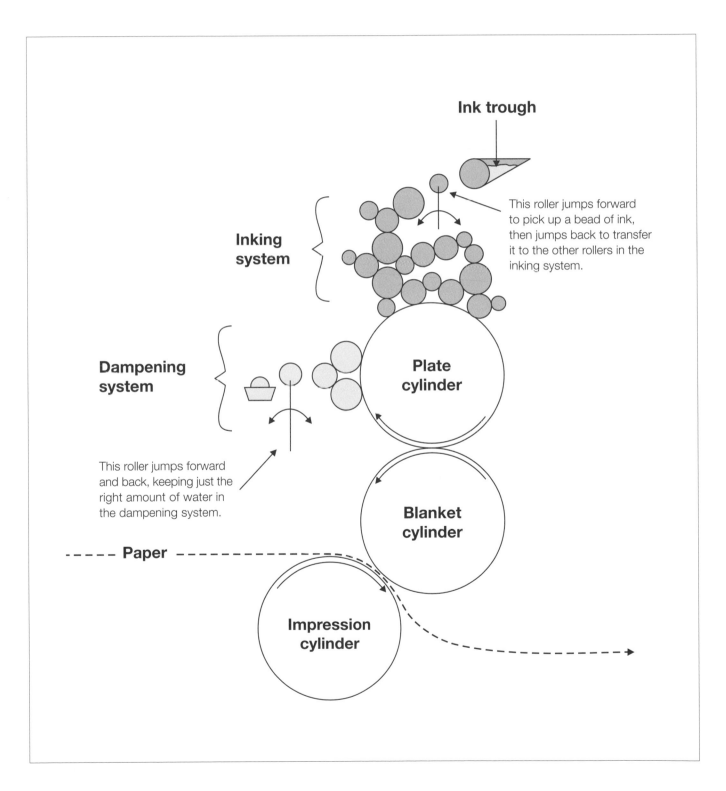

Ink trough

Inking system

This roller jumps forward to pick up a bead of ink, then jumps back to transfer it to the other rollers in the inking system.

Dampening system

Plate cylinder

This roller jumps forward and back, keeping just the right amount of water in the dampening system.

Blanket cylinder

Paper

Impression cylinder

Other Printing Methods

As I have said, this book is primarily concerned with sheet-fed offset litho, but graphic designers may also be asked to work with one of the other industrial printing mediums. Here is a brief description of the four most common of them.

Web offset litho

Web offset litho relies on the same kind of process used by sheet-fed offset litho with one notable difference: instead of printing sheets, it prints a continuous roll, or web. It is therefore capable of incredible speed and commonly prints both sides of the sheet in the same pass, a process called **perfecting**.

Web machines can be frightening not only in terms of size and noise level – some are as tall as a two- or three-storey building and sound like an express train – but also in terms of how fast the hapless designer who is proofing the job on-press has to make decisions.

As the web leaves the last ink unit, it is folded and then cut into sheets as part of the 'in-line' process, and this, of course, means that the ink on the paper must be absolutely dry. Infrared or even propane dryers are commonly mounted between each ink unit to ensure that all the colours have set before the folding begins. An exception to this is newsprint, which uses **cold-set inks**. These are formulated to dry very quickly on absorbent paper stocks.

Because of the speed of production, web inks are thinner than those used for sheet-fed work. Dot gain levels (see Chapter 4) are therefore different – roughly double those of sheet-fed. They also sometimes vary from press to press even within the same shop, so be sure to check with the printer before finally calibrating any images.

Flexography

This method is mainly used for packaging. The plates, which are made of a rubber compound, look as if they have been etched as the surface stands out from the background. In fact, **flexography** plates are usually made in a mould. Because of their flexibility and three-dimensional surface the plates tend to 'squish' somewhat under the pressure of transferring the ink to the page. This means that small dots can get considerably bigger, and dot gain levels can therefore be serious. Registration tends to be rather looser than with offset litho, but a plus is the ability to print onto non-absorbent surfaces such as plastic and metal. If you are going to print using this method, talk to your printer about the kind of images you want to include in the job before you put everything together. Definitely ask about dot gain,

screen density and registration tolerances, which can vary considerably from shop to shop. Although small type and fine screens are normally to be avoided when using flexography, there are specialist printers in the field who can produce things like 4pt type and four-colour 133-line screens beautifully.

Screenprinting

Imagine a mesh stretched across a wooden frame that has then been placed face down on a table. That is the idea of a 'screen' in **screenprinting**. Of course, the frame is much more likely to be made of metal, and the screen is much more likely to be a very fine polyester or metal mesh, but the basic idea is the same.

Ink is poured onto the mesh along one of the edges of the frame. The screen, which is a porous membrane, carries on it the image background, which acts as a non-porous stencil. As the ink is pulled across the membrane by a rubber-edged squeegee, ink is forced through the porous areas – i.e. the image – and onto the page beneath. Then the frame is lifted, leaving the page behind. It is removed, a new one is put into its place, the frame comes down again and the ink is squeegeed back across it.

Of course, the 'page' used in screenprinting is quite often something like a T-shirt, but this method is also used for physically large pages on very small runs – for instance, shop signs. The appropriate images can be printed, one frame at a time, across a 5-metre (16-foot) sheet of the material from which the sign is being made.

The methods by which the image is created on the screen vary enormously. At one end of the scale, the image can be painted onto the screen by hand. At the other, a photo-sensitive material is bonded to the mesh onto which the image is generated, in much the same way that offset-litho plates are made, i.e. from an exposure through a sheet of film that carries the image, or even by direct exposure to laser.

Screenprinting is not a method that lends itself to very fine detail, and sometimes the mesh of the screen can add a new twist to trying to avoid **moiré patterns** in four-colour work. But obviously there are areas into which screenprinters can go that other printing methods cannot reach. Screenprinting is not always a manual operation. There are also fully automated systems in use that can provide much faster and more consistent results.

Gravure

Gravure (or Rotogravure) is the printing method that makes banknotes so hard to forge. It uses either a diamond-etched copper plate or a laser-etched polymer resin plate; either way, the printing process is the same.

Gravure plates are very thick compared to those of sheet-fed and web offset. Instead of the ink adhering to the portions of the plate that are left as a raised surface, gravure plates rely on using a much thinner ink that fills the 'cells' etched into it. The deeper the cell, the more ink can be held – and the darker the corresponding dot on the paper. Excess ink is continually wiped off the raised surfaces of the revolving plate by a steel blade.

Because the ink is thinner, it spreads when it hits the page. This means that the printed result appears to be a continuous tone. This makes gravure the highest-quality option for image reproduction, but conversely a lower-quality option for type, which will also be made up of the same kind of cells as the image.

Originally, gravure cells were all of equal size but varying depths, but it is now possible to use cells of varying size as well. Gravure platemaking is extremely expensive, and as it is also a web printing process it is much more involved (and therefore more expensive) to set up and run than a simple sheet-fed press. As a result, gravure is usually suited only to extremely long press runs.

An environmental note

Whichever method you choose, printing is a messy business. It can also be highly toxic. Film chemicals are nasty, as are some used for developing plates, while inks can contain all sorts of heavy metals, and the solvents used to remove them afterwards are usually varying grades of jet aircraft fuel. So, if possible, encourage your printer to use a more environmentally friendly system. Both water-developing plates and soy-based inks are available, and a computer-to-plate system completely avoids the use of film. Also, try to use recycled paper whenever possible: a single weekend edition of the *New York Times* requires the wood from more than fifty acres of forest (fig. **1.11**).

Do not assume that the kind of paper you want is not made in a recycled stock – the range available today is huge. Just call your printers and talk to them.

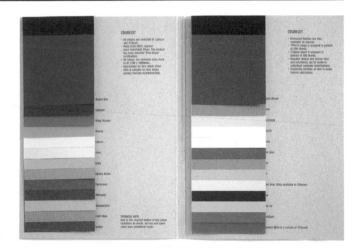

1.11 A swatch of recycled paper samples. Recycled stock is available almost everywhere.

Four-Colour Printing Explained

Anyone intending to send colour work to a printer needs to understand the 'four-colour process', the means by which their work will be reproduced. These four ink colours are cyan, magenta, yellow and black, and the set is collectively known as 'CMYK'. However, in a typical colour photo there will be thousands of colours, not four. And even in a single-colour image, there are many, many shades.

However, the printer can only use these four colours to reproduce the entire range required by a colour photo; and in a black-and-white photo the printer can only use black to create all the apparent shades of grey. Clearly there has to be some technology involved to help things along.

This chapter deals with how the four-colour process works so that you can understand its limitations, and therefore begin to overcome some of them. In addition to the restricted range of colours you can create with CMYK, there are screen angles to think about... and screen clash too, of course... better read on!

Opposite: A colour separation shown in cyan, magenta, yellow and black, each screened to the appropriate angle to ensure successful printing.

A Word about Paper Weights and Sizes

The US and the UK use different paper sizes and calculate paper 'weight' (which usually indicates thickness) differently. Paper also has a grain. It is similar to the grain in wood, and is caused by the tendency of the individual paper fibres to line up along the length of the manufactured roll rather than across it. All these are factors to consider when choosing stock.

In the UK, the most common sizes of sheet are based on one called 'AO', which covers a total of one square metre and measures 841 x 1189mm (33⅛ x 46¾in). This can be cut in half along the long edge to produce an A1 sheet, which is 841 x 594mm (33⅛ x 23⅜in). This can be cut in half in the same way to produce an A2, which is 420 x 594mm (16½ x 23⅜in), and so on. An A4, the standard letter-sized sheet, measures 210mm (8¼in) wide x 297mm (11¾in) tall.

Sheet thickness is based on the weight of a one-metre square; therefore, an A4 page could be 90gsm (grams per square metre) or 130gsm, which would be correspondingly thicker.

Sometimes paper is made fluffier in order to give it added opacity, as in the case of many paperback books. In this case, its weight might be the same as a similar sheet that has been compressed further, but its thickness would be greater.

Of course, printers usually need to print on something *larger* than an A4 page in order to end up *giving* you an A4 page. The extra space allows for registration marks, printer's marks (blocks of varying tints used to measure ink density) or trim marks. So there are two additional size standards, based on the 'A' series, which include a set amount of 'trim', the area into which those things useful to a printer can be placed. The smaller of the two adds 'R' to the page-size formula (for instance, an RA4 measures 215 x 305mm/8¼ x 12in), and allows for a very small trim. The larger is the 'SR' series (as in SRA4, measuring 225 x 320mm/ 8¾ x 12⅝in), which gives the printer a bit more space to allow for more information. The SR series is generally easier for printers to work with, and enables them to produce a higher-quality end product.

There are two other standard sheet sizes in the UK, the 'B' and 'C' series. A BO sheet measures 1000 x 1414 mm (39⅜ x 55⅝in), and is halved to produce a B1 of 1000 x 707mm (39⅜ x 27⅞in) and so on. A CO sheet is 917 x 1297mm (36⅛ x 51in) and halves to give a C1 of 917 x 648mm (36⅛ x 25½in), etc. Note that when halving the long edge dimension of any of these standard sizes produces an odd half millimetre, it is rounded down to the next full number.

In the US, the situation is rather more complicated. Paper falls into three basic groups: text (also called 'book') papers; cover stocks; and a group combining 'bond', 'writing' and 'ledger' paper. Sizes for all these are measured in inches, and weights are calculated in terms of how many pounds (lb) 500 sheets (one 'ream') of the 'parent' size stock weigh. For text and book papers, the weight is calculated on a ream of parent sheets measuring 25 x 38in. Cover stocks are based on a parent size of 20 x 26in, writing papers on 17 x 22in, and bond and ledger sheets on 19 x 24in. In addition to those, there is also a range of card stocks – used for postcards, for example – that are not measured in terms of weight but in thickness. A typical postcard might be described as 10-point C1S ('C1S' translates as 'coated one side'), meaning not that it is as thick as a 10pt type character but that its thickness is $^{10}/_{1000}$ in.

The standard letter size in the US is 8½ x 11in. Many other standard sizes are available, based on the parent size. For example, a text sheet might be described as an 80lb stock measuring 19 x 25in. Cover stock, which is of course usually heavier, might be given as 60lb and measure 20 x 26in. In both these instances, the second dimension also indicates the **grain direction**. Therefore a 19 x 25in sheet cannot actually be cut from one measuring 25 x 38in, but it could be cut from one measuring 38 x 25in.

Envelopes can be a real pain. Although there are many different standard sizes, the likelihood of finding the size you want in the stock you want can be slim. If you are designing a job that requires an envelope, think ahead and prepare to be flexible. As you will invariably be asking your printer to order stock for you, it is generally better to check up on envelope availability – and paper, too, if you intend to choose anything that is not fairly run-of-the-mill – and then design the job around stock that you know is available.

To produce your work, the printer will need to purchase sheets of one of the standard sizes. This may be cut down for the press, or used straight out of the package. If you specify an odd page size, it may mean that there is much more 'spoilage' – i.e. a higher proportion of the page will have to be cut off and discarded – than if you use something closer to a standard. In such cases, you should not only expect a higher paper cost, you should be aware that you might be asking the printer to work harder than normal. For example, non-standard sizes and orientations can mean a more difficult job for the folder; this means more sheets will be damaged, therefore more will need to be ordered. Also, as paper folds more easily with the grain than against it, heavier stocks that also require folding will either be ordered so that the grain goes with the fold, or an additional score will be added.

Imposition

If you are interested only in printing single images such as posters, **imposition** will not affect you. But any time you are printing a multiple-page piece it becomes very important. Imposition is the name given to the configuration in which the pages are positioned on the larger press sheet, enabling the job to run cost-effectively through the printer, folder and binder.

If you know the basic rules of imposition, you will be able to configure your work to be more efficient. For example, each side of a sheet of paper counts as a page. Therefore a single sheet would be a two-page insert in a book – but there is no way to include a single sheet other than by physically glueing it into place close to the spine, or making it slightly wider than a regular page so that it can be bound in, leaving a narrow and unsightly tab adjacent to the binding. Either way, it is an undesirable result.

In order to avoid this situation, multiple-page jobs should always be calculated to generate a page count that is a multiple of four, eight or (best of all if it is possible) sixteen. As each **signature** (i.e. each separate sheet that, when printed and folded, will be bound together as a book/magazine/newsletter) requires individual handling, if you can end up with two sixteen-page signatures it is a more efficient way of producing a book than ending up with one sixteen-page, one eight-page and one four-page signature, even though the latter has a smaller total page count. With two sixteen-page signatures, the folder has to be set up only once to deal with the whole job. With the latter scenario, three separate set-ups are required on the folder and three pick-ups instead of two are needed to collect the signatures together for binding. Of course, that does not mean you should just stick with two sixteen-page signatures even though it will mean four blank pages at the end of the book. It just means that you have to bear in mind what is best for the job.

The way the pages are positioned within the configuration of a single signature depends on the size of the press (which limits the number of pages it is possible to place on a single plate), the total number of pages in the publication, and the way in which it is being bound. As an example, let us take an eight-page newsletter and a plate size that can handle all eight pages together. It will then be folded and **saddle-stitched**, i.e. stapled along the fold, and trimmed on three sides. To see how the pages will need to be imposed, take a single A4 sheet of paper. Fold it in half, and it becomes a four-page signature. Fold it in half again, and it is an eight-page signature. Take a pen and number the loose corners (and in only one of the four corners of the folded sheet will there be eight loose corners) from 1 to 8. When you unfold the page, the result should look like fig. **2.1**. Side one

will carry numbers 1, 8, 4 and 5; side two will have numbers 2, 7, 6 and 3. Incidentally, this is called a **folding dummy**, and is a very useful thing to include with the **laser proofs** you send to the printer.

The way the printer would want to set this up is called a **work-and-turn format**, in which side one of a four-page section occupies the left-hand half of the plate, and side two occupies the right-hand half. The press sheet is then printed, picking up both images. Then it is turned over (fig. **2.2**) and run through again. The result is two complete eight-page signatures, one on each half of the press sheet.

One of the advantages of using the work-and-turn format is that the press can grab the sheet along the same gripper edge for both print runs. This means that the image on one side can be registered to the image on the reverse very accurately, even if the paper has been cut slightly out of square at the mill, as is often the case. If the press sheets are printed using a **work-and-tumble format**, in which the sheets are turned over along the short edge instead, the gripper edge changes. This can make it much more difficult – or even impossible – to properly register both sides of the job to each other. Therefore, the paper for a work-and-tumble press run is usually 'cut square' beforehand, i.e. trimmed slightly to ensure that each corner is exactly 90 degrees.

An instance of a job requiring a work-and-tumble press run is given in fig. **2.3**. This shows both sides of a ten-panel brochure, with the panels positioned so that when the sheets are tumbled, the five reverse panels will back up the five panels on the front side, again producing two brochures from each press sheet. Of the two configurations, printers definitely prefer to use work-and-turn.

There is a third possible printing configuration called **sheetwise**. In a sheetwise run, separate plates are needed to print both sides of the sheet. This could be because only one side of the job can fit on the plate (for example, a large poster) or because the requirements of one side of the sheet will not allow for a work-and-turn or a work-and-tumble format – as in a postcard run, for instance, where four colours will be printed on one side of the sheet but only one colour on the reverse.

Binding can affect imposition placement, depending on whether the signatures will be collected one inside the other and then saddle-stitched, as for a magazine, or collected side by side and then sewn or glued together, as for a hardcover or paperback book. As each successive signature is gathered for saddle-stitching, the thickness of the paper builds up along the binding and pushes those signatures towards the centre of

2.1 (Below, Left and Right) Both sides of an unfolded eight-page signature, showing page numbering.

2.2 (Bottom Left) An eight-page signature set up on a plate as a work-and-turn. The shaded area along the top of the sheet indicates the gripper edge. Additional space for a trim has been added above and below the horizontal fold across the centre of the sheet. This allows the fold to be trimmed off without affecting the intended page size.

2.3 (Bottom Right) A work-and-tumble press sheet. Typically, a work-and-tumble is used only for jobs that are impossible to print as a work-and-turn, as in this case – a ten-panel brochure.

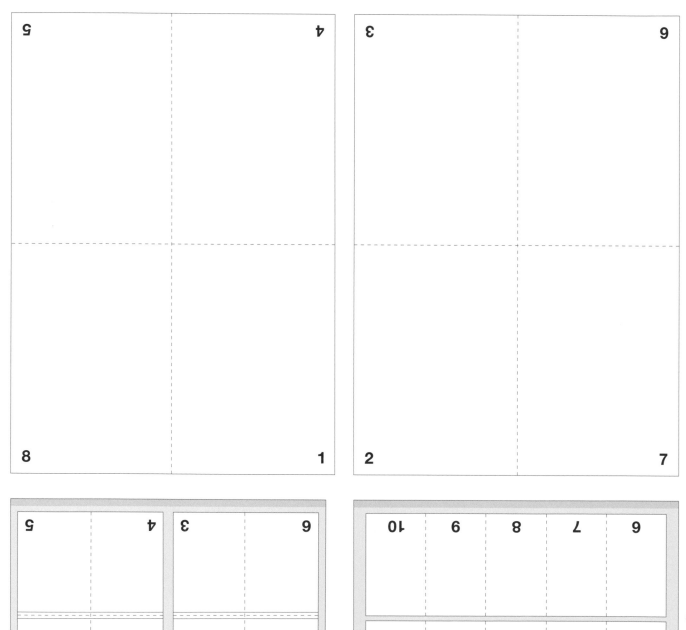

CMY... K?

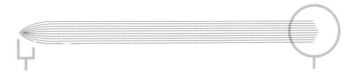

2.4 Saddle-stitched publications are prone to 'creep': displacement caused by a build-up of paper along the binding.

2.5 From left to right, cyan, magenta, yellow and black: the CMYK colours.

the publication further and further out (fig. **2.4**). This is known as **creep**, and can be adjusted for during the imposition process. Signatures gathered side by side do not create the same kind of build-up, so the problem does not arise.

Most graphic designers know that the inks used in four-colour process printing are cyan, magenta, yellow and black (CMYK) (fig. **2.5**). While it is reasonable to abbreviate cyan, magenta and yellow to C, M and Y, how come black is given the letter K? Here is how I found out.

Towards the end of my very first day working in the printing industry, one of the printers told me that he needed a new 'key plate' first thing the next morning. I had no idea what he meant and thought he was joking. When I eventually arrived an hour after him the following day, he was not happy, to say the least.

This was not good. When the presses stop, the shop is no longer printing money. A new key plate, I was rapidly informed, is a plate that prints the colour that all the other colours key to: black. If you think about it, it is obvious. Text and image borders are typically printed in black. Printing them first often makes it easier to position – or 'key' – the other colours to the job. So 'key' is actually what the 'K' stands for.

It is a common misconception that black is assigned the letter 'K' because if it were called 'B' it could be confused with blue. While plausible, this is not the case.

Screen Angles
and Screen Clash

As we have already seen (in Chapter 1), if you want to print a photograph using black ink, you used to have to break it up into dots by bouncing the image through a screen and on to film. Alternatively, you can use software like Adobe Photoshop together with digital cameras and/or scanners to capture the image, and then the imagesetter (the machine that outputs plates or film from your files) **rasterizes** the result, i.e. turns all the **pixel** information into halftone dots. Whichever method you use, screen or software, the end result is an illusion of an image that is actually made up of a grid of dots arranged in a grid of lines at 90° to each other.

This is why at a print shop they do not talk about dots so much as about the lines of dots that together make up a screen of dots. It is not a 150-dot halftone; it is a 150 'line screen' halftone. Different press technologies and papers can handle only certain densities of screen, so the decision as to which one you use is important. But more of that later.

Printing the first colour is no problem. But what happens when you want to print an image in more than one colour? That means you are planning to print two screens of dots, one on top of the other. The results can be quite a surprise:

Colour 1, black (fig. **2.6**).

Colour 2, cyan (fig. **2.7**).

Now let us look at them together: fig. **2.8**. This unfortunate result is called a moiré pattern. It is caused when two screens are laid down at close to the same angle and clash. Every few lines, the dots collide. However, printers discovered that if the second screen is turned until the rows of dots are 30° away from the first, the problem goes away (fig. **2.9**).

So, colour 1 can appear with a screen angle of 0° and 90° – i.e. the rows of dots are arranged on a grid of horizontal and vertical lines. Colour 2 is turned 30° away from it. Colour 3 has to be turned 30° away from both of them. So far, this is what you have (fig. **2.10**).

Given that the colours need to be separated by 30° spaces, where can you put colour number 4? There is simply nowhere for it to go. If you rotate it another 30°, you are back to where you started – on 0° and 90°. Fortunately, the answer lies in the nature of the colours themselves.

Consider the way we see colours. Obviously enough, we see black as the darkest and yellow as the lightest, while cyan and magenta fall somewhere in between. When any one of them is printed as a fine screen (around 150 lines to the inch),

2.6 Colour 1, black.

2.7 Colour 2, cyan.

2.8 A moiré pattern.

2.9 The two colours together but at non-conflicting screen angles.

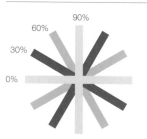

2.10 Three of the CMYK components separated by 30° increments.

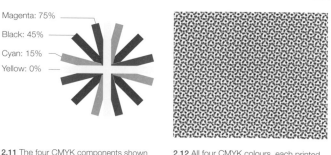

Magenta: 75%
Black: 45%
Cyan: 15%
Yellow: 0%

2.11 The four CMYK components shown at the correct screen angles for printing.

2.12 All four CMYK colours, each printed as a screen at the correct angle.

Beyond Four Colours

the dots are so small that we cannot see them even if we hold the sheet only 250–300mm (10–12in) away from us. Yellow is even harder to distinguish. It is so invisible to us that we have not even noticed it causing a moiré pattern in every four-colour print we have ever seen. And yet that is exactly what it does. Yellow can slide in between any two of the other colours, only 15° away from both of them. It always causes a moiré, and we never, ever, see it. But this is not the case with any of the other colours.

Printers take things even further. As well as there being a range of relative visibility in the colours themselves, there are more- and less-visible screen angles. Not surprisingly, the most visible orientations – the ones that we will see more easily than any of the others – are 0° and 90°. When you think about it, it makes perfect sense. Our world is filled with vertical and horizontal objects, so we are especially used to noticing those angles.

Yellow, the least visible colour, goes in at 0° (or 90°), the most visible angle.

Black, the most visible colour, goes in at 45°, the least visible angle.

Magenta and cyan are placed 30° either side of black, one at 15° and the other at 75° – and it does not matter which of them goes where (fig. **2.11**).

Remember, all of this is simply intended to maintain the illusion. That is all you need to do.

When these print as a screen of dots, and each colour is set at the correct angle, there is no visible moiré pattern at all (fig. **2.12**). And that is the secret of the four-colour process.

There are two leaders in the evolution of colour technology. One is the use of **stochastic** or **frequency-modulated screens**. As already mentioned, in a conventional halftone the dots are locked into a grid pattern. Therefore, in order to display (the illusion of) different shades of a colour, they have to vary in size. However, on an inkjet printer all the dots are the same size. In order for them to convey the same illusion, they cannot be locked into a grid. Instead, they are sprayed apparently at random at varying densities. Because there are no grids to cause screen clash, the image is no longer subject to moiré patterns. Therefore any number of colours can be added to extend the range well beyond that of CMYK inks.

The disadvantages of the process are mostly in dealing with the extremely small dots needed to create a convincing image. If the dots are too big, the result looks grainy, even though the dots are actually much smaller than those in a conventional halftone. If the dots are too small, even a tiny amount of dot gain can wipe them out altogether, or make them repeatedly plug up on the press.

Some imagesetters can produce 'hexachrome' (i.e. six-colour) separations using stochastic screens of around 600**dpi** (dots per inch, actually meaning pixels per inch, the accepted measurement of image resolution), good enough for a high-quality print. In hexachrome separations, orange and green are added to the CMYK range in order to extend those areas that are most difficult to duplicate conventionally.

The other 'next step' also uses hexachrome separations, but in a different way. The two additional colours, orange and green, are the opposites of cyan and magenta, respectively. Therefore, any given colour will contain only one of the pair – orange or cyan; green or magenta – but not both. This means that both colours in each pair can occupy the same screen angle, because they never actually occupy the same space within the image. Thus they do not create a moiré pattern, making it possible to use conventional halftone screening with a six-colour hexachrome process instead of CMYK's four.

Pantone Inc. is pioneering the development of this system, and claims that more than 90% of its **Pantone Matching System** colour range can be matched using hexachrome inks (see Chapter 10). This will allow graphic designers to get much closer in print to colours that, so far, they have only been able to work with on screen in RGB images. An advantage to printers is that, instead of washing one custom-mixed ink after another off the press, they will be able to stay with the six hexachrome colours for almost everything.

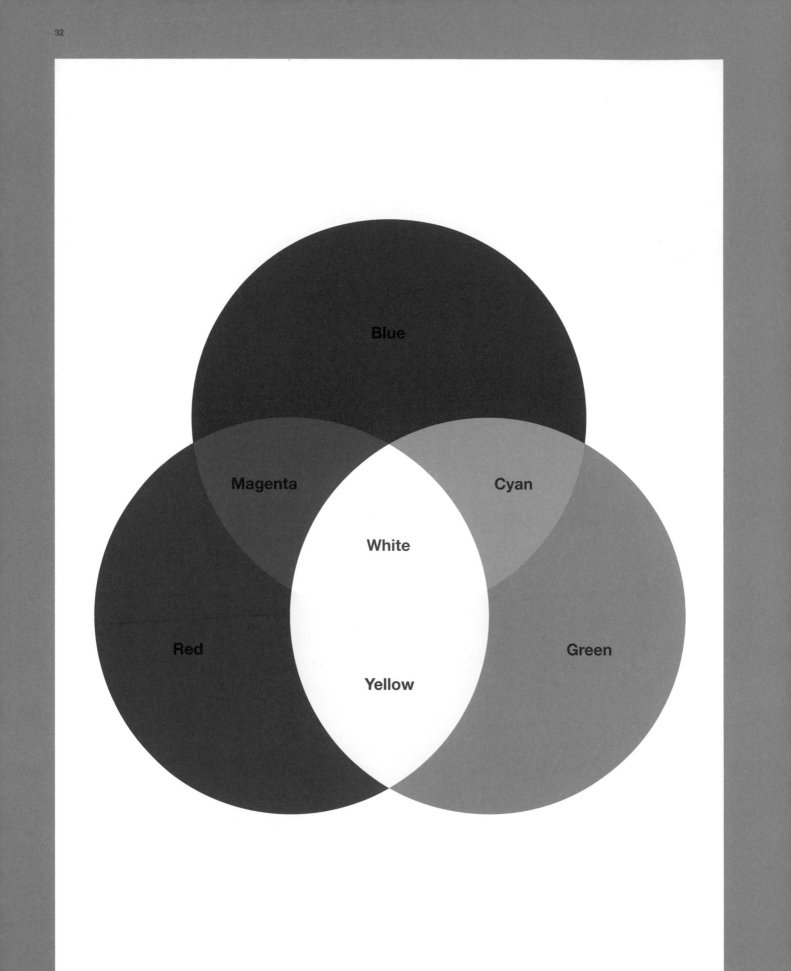

Understanding Colour

Wonderful though computers are, and despite having streamlined the entire production process for graphic designers everywhere, they have certain limitations. For instance, computer monitors can only show us images in 'RGB' (red, green and blue) colour. It is vitally important to understand this and how it relates to CMYK, because only then can we hope to avoid the biggest problem in the print industry today, which is the client saying, 'those are not the colours I was expecting'.

Anything you see on your screen is RGB, a very wide colour spectrum. Anything you see in print is reproduced using CMYK (or with Pantone colours, see Chapter 10), which is, alas, quite a narrow spectrum. Therefore, what you see on your screen may be a long way from what you will see in the printed result.

Getting the colours you want using CMYK is not always easy, and sometimes impossible. However, avoiding possible disaster is *always* possible, as long as you understand colour.

Opposite: A colour wheel showing the relationship between RGB and CMYK colour spaces.

RGB vs. CMYK

The main reason I decided to write this book is because so many of my students have had the miserable experience of sending their files to the printer and getting back something that is radically different in colour from what they were expecting. They know something is seriously wrong, but they have no idea what it is – and therefore cannot fix it.

This chapter discusses what is wrong, and how to begin fixing it. To start with, let us have a closer look at RGB and CMYK.

First, what does RGB mean? R is red, G is green, B is blue. You probably knew that already, but would you know how to get yellow using RGB? It is extremely difficult to think in terms of RGB, and yet that is the method your computer uses to display every single colour. RGB is the format that scanners and digital cameras use, too. So, all the images you see on your computer start out in RGB format, regardless of what is done to them afterwards. There is just no getting away from it.

We saw in the last chapter how the CMYK colours work, so surely that is the most important format to know about when sending files off for printing. If that is the case, do you really need to bother about RGB? The answer is yes, because unless you know what to avoid, and how to avoid it, RGB will forever be getting in your way, and you will never feel confident about whether you will obtain the printed colours you want.

It will not work merely to change everything into CMYK as soon as it is on screen – even though it is essential that everything you eventually send to the printer is in CMYK format (unless it is a multi-channel 'extension' of CMYK that also contains spot-colour information – see the 'DCS' section of Chapter 7). So, while the change to CMYK does need to be made, it is that change, and the way in which it occurs, that usually causes the problems.

The first thing we need to understand is that RGB refers to different colours of light, whereas CMYK refers to different colours of pigment. We have all developed some level of understanding about the way pigments mix together from the time someone first gave us a paintbrush and a box of paints. If there is a colour we need but do not have, we probably have a good idea of how we might create it using the 'primary' colours. These are colours that cannot themselves be mixed, but from which we can mix a whole range of 'secondary' colours. For instance, if we want green – a secondary colour – we would mix together the primary colours blue and yellow. For purple, we would mix blue and red. For orange, yellow and red, and so on.

All the paints we have ever used share this characteristic, and CMYK is just a particularly limited range of paints: we get only four colours, and everything else we need has to be mixed from them.

RGB is, in a way, even more limited because there are only three colours in the palette. Yet these colours mix in such a different way that it is possible to obtain a much wider range of colours from them than from CMYK. Unfortunately, many graphic designers have no idea about what the result will be when they mix RGB colours, because nobody ever gave them a paintbox containing colours made of light.

As well as being fundamentally different colour systems, there is another big problem with CMYK vs. RGB. RGB is *almost* the exact opposite of CMYK, but not quite, and that is the cause of many colour-related problems for the graphic designer. By the end of this chapter I hope you will understand what I mean by 'almost exact opposites'.

CMYK and RGB are different in other ways, too. Because they are made of light, RGB colours can be seen in the dark. CMYK colours, being made up of pigments, cannot.

CMYK is called a 'subtractive' system because the C, M and Y components in theory combine to absorb all light and produce black. Of course, in practice, they do not. RGB is called an 'additive' system, because it does (almost) the opposite.

Can you trust your monitor?

If you have ever had the experience of having an image that looks a certain way on screen, but then prints to look radically different, your lack of control over the change from RGB to CMYK is extremely likely to be the reason. However, it may not be the only reason. If you decide it is a calibration issue, read Chapter 4 for greyscale, and Chapter 6 for colour images.

When you convert an image from RGB to CMYK mode, your monitor has no choice but to display the new CMYK version using RGB colours. So, an additional problem is that, as far as final printed colour is concerned, *your monitor cannot be trusted.*

Incidentally, there is a very small range of colours within the CMYK range that you cannot produce with RGB. Pure cyan is one of them. So is pure yellow. But do not worry. Strangely enough, even though these are two of the primary CMYK colours, it is very unlikely to be a problem. Problems are much more likely to be caused by being unable to create an RGB colour using CMYK than the other way around.

Colour Opposites

Taking a quick look at how colour photography works is a good way to gain a better understanding of the differences between RGB and CMYK.

If we take a picture, the colours coming in through the lens are made up of light, not pigment. So, the input information (light) is RGB format rather than CMYK. However, when using film, light hits the film and causes the chemical emulsions on its surface to react. Those chemicals result in colours that are much closer to the pigments used in CMYK than to those found in RGB. When the film is developed (print film, not slides), the end result is a colour negative of the image that came in through the lens.

If we examine a film negative we will see that when we take a picture of something magenta, the resulting image on the film negative is green. If we photograph something orange, the resulting image is blue. If the tone was light, the resulting image on the film is dark. Every part of the image on the film is the opposite of what we actually photographed.

Then, to get a positive print, an exposure is made through the image onto photographic print paper. White light is projected through the film and becomes tinted by all the colours in the negative image. If it goes through a green area, the light that travels through to the photographic paper beneath it has picked up a green tint, which then develops to give us the opposite – a magenta area. And so on. The end result is usually a very convincing picture of whatever we were pointing the camera at when we took the shot.

So, even in a camera, the colours created by light and those created by pigments act as opposites. By using their understanding of this fundamental difference, photographers and printers have been able to develop some incredibly sophisticated methods to achieve the exact results they want.

The same kind of understanding can be used by a designer to obtain the desired results in print.

Early developers of the CMYK system had to work with the opposites of RGB because pigments of red, green and blue are a hopelessly inadequate palette by themselves. It is impossible to mix them to create anything close to the range of colours required to print a photographic image. But their opposites work very well.

Cyan is as close as we can get, in pigment form, to the opposite of the red in RGB. Magenta is as close as we can get to the opposite of RGB green. Yellow is closest to the opposite of RGB blue. But none of them are exact opposites.

If you wanted to create white with CMYK, you would simply leave them all out. If you wanted to do the same thing using RGB, you would include them all at 100%. In that example,

RGB and CMYK act as exact opposites of each other. But what happens when we try to create black?

It seems obvious, at least for the CMYK part of the equation: do not bother with the C, M or Y, but use plenty of K.

The thing is, if the two systems were exact opposites, we would be able to get black using just C, M and Y. But we cannot, and that is why black had to be added as a fourth colour – because you simply cannot create it with C, M and Y.

So, by their natures, the two systems are exact opposites when it comes to creating white, but they are not exact opposites when it comes to creating black. That is what I mean when I say they are 'almost exact' opposites. To sum up:

Question: How do we get black using RGB?
Answer: We turn off all of the colours (in other words, we turn off the lights).

Question: How do we get black using C, M and Y?
Answer: It is not possible. The combination of the three, even at full strength, is not dark enough to be convincing. That is why we have to include black.

Actually, it is debatable whether we can even get black with black. When I was at art college, a friend announced that his forthcoming masterpiece was to be a huge canvas painted black. The result, far from being a laughing matter, was quite a shock. The canvas was indeed painted black – but had first been divided into big squares, and each square then filled with a different 'black' medium. Oil paint, water paint, poster paint, ink... all the usual 'black' pigments were there – but also boot polish, stove paint, soot and even a black plastic sheet.

Looking at the finished work, all the 'blacks' appeared to have a particular colour tint. The black plastic was obviously blue; the soot, in comparison, looked slightly red. And so on. This was a major revelation for me: colour is relative, and you cannot see black when you still have the lights on. (Even with the lights off you would not really see black. Your eyes will not let you, only flickerings here and there.)

To take another example, try looking at something that is black. The only reason you can see it is because it is reflecting light into your eyes. That is the basis of your visual image. And if it is reflecting light, if you can see definition and shading, then you cannot be seeing something that is perfectly black – because true black could only appear in the total absence of light. It is an absence of reflection, definition and shading. In other words, black is a very profound state of 'lights off'.

When it comes to printing, you have to use something as close to true black as possible because, as previously mentioned, you cannot create anything really close to it with just cyan, magenta and yellow. The pigment used is usually carbon, which makes black the cheapest of all the ink colours. And of course, while it is not really black, that is what we all call it. While its inclusion is essential, a typical four-colour separation will contain less black than it will of the other three colours. Black tends to be found around clearly defined edges – it is what helps define them – and of course you will find it in the deep shadows. But there probably will not be very much of it anywhere else. On the other hand, cyan, magenta and yellow will usually be present at higher densities throughout the entire tonal range of the image.

Aside from the need for it in images, black is obviously useful for other things as well – type, for example.

Now that we have some idea how the two systems compare, let us try to create yellow with both of them. Incidentally, in the formula shown in fig. **3.1**, the 'K' is in parentheses because it is only included to enable the CMYK range to extend to 'black' and dark colours close to it. As yellow is the lightest colour in the range, K will not be needed at all.

C	0%	100%	R
M	0%	100%	G
Y	100%	0%	B
(K)	0%		

3.1 How to mix yellow using RGB and CMYK colours. This shows the opposing nature of the two colour systems.

I mentioned earlier that (CMYK) cyan and (RGB) red are more or less opposites, as are (CMYK) magenta and (RGB) green, as are (CMYK) yellow and (RGB) blue.

Handily enough, the combination of (RGB) red and (RGB) green is also the opposite of (RGB) blue. Similarly, the combination of (CMYK) cyan and (CMYK) magenta is the opposite of (CMYK) yellow. So, in order to get yellow out of C, M and Y, we turn on Y, but we also have to make sure that we turn off C and M. In RGB, the opposite system, we turn on R and G, and we also have to turn off B.

Try playing around with this in the Colour Picker window in Photoshop. Click on the foreground colour to open the window, and in the RGB area enter a value of 255 for R and G, and 0 for B. The result is yellow. Then try entering 255 for R and B and the result is magenta. And entering 255 for G and B gives

you cyan. So the RGB system contains C, M and Y as secondary combinations of its three primaries. Then try the same using the C, M and Y of the CMYK area. A combination of 100% cyan and magenta will give you as close to RGB blue as you can get using pigments. It looks like a dark purple. If you enter 100% for magenta and yellow, you will get the pigment version of RGB red. It is red, but nowhere near as bright or saturated as RGB red. Last, try 100% of yellow and cyan. The result is the CMYK version of RGB green – a long way from RGB green, but again as close as CMYK can get. So the CMYK system also contains versions of the RGB colours as secondary combinations of its primaries, although they are fairly dull and drab when compared to the RGB versions. This means it is very tempting to use something bright, saturated and RGB when we create colours on screen.

So, it is the differences between RGB and CMYK that are most important, because they are what cause the problems. The combination of 100% cyan and 100% magenta might look completely different and less interesting than pure RGB blue, which we are therefore tempted to pick instead, but it is as close as CMYK can get. Most designers do not really take that seriously enough, so they merrily send RGB colours off to the printer. The result, of course, is a total disaster.

How You Perceive Colour

Understanding and remembering the relative nature of colour is hugely important because it keeps us aware of the bigger picture, all the time. For a designer, the bigger picture might be the whole page rather than just one of the images on it; the whole project rather than just that single page; and the entire environment in which the work will exist rather than just the process that led up to its delivery to the client.

So, what colour is a green leaf in a dark room? And why is this important?

Right now, you might feel that the leaf stays green, even in the dark. If so, see if the following example changes your mind.

If you think about it, the only things our eyes can see are colour and shape. Both depend on light. Everything we see depends on the presence of light. So far we can all agree. But the colour of what we see depends on the colour of the light. A leaf only looks green if the light shining on it is white. It absorbs all the other colours and reflects green, and in our minds the green-ness and the leaf-ness somehow become one thing. But that is not accurate at all. If it were, then no matter what we did to it, the leaf would stay green. Yet if we shine a red light on it, there is no green to reflect at us, because red light does not contain a green element. Suddenly the leaf looks very dark, almost black. But the leaf itself has not changed at all. The only thing that has changed is the light, which bounces off the leaf as impartially as it does everything else within range.

There is no fundamental, inherent light source that is more valid than any other light source, despite what whole civilizations have thought about the sun until now. It is just that we are used to the sun hanging around up above us every day, and the lights we have in our houses are designed to be similar in colour. And so we have come to feel the most comfortable with the way our world appears when it is illuminated with a whitish source of light. White light contains all the colours of the visible spectrum, so the objects it illuminates reflect the widest possible visible range. That is why things look more 'real' to us when illuminated by white light than by a light of any other colour. However, the fact that we prefer the way things look when illuminated by white light is just a habit based on how we are used to seeing things. A leaf is not inherently green. Or red. Or anything. Its colour is relative, and depends on other equally relative factors for all its apparently inherent characteristics, just like everything else. In the case of the green leaf, if there is no light it is impossible to talk about its colour, because the factor on which the appearance of colour depends is not present (fig. **3.2**).

3.2 If the 'green leaf' example was confusing, try this. On the left: a green leaf. On the right: so what colour is it now?

A Case Study

Now that the basics of RGB and CMYK have been covered, let us have a look at a practical example of the kind of problem you might encounter with them.

Some years ago, at a print shop in Cumbria, England, an excellent designer (Charlie) was asked to put together a brochure for a company that specialized in designing and building unmanned submarines. In creating a design for them, Charlie made two very big mistakes.

First mistake: Charlie decided to use two shades of blue, readily available in Photoshop, to create a full-bleed graduated tint as a background for the whole brochure. This would look like an underwater shot of the ocean on which the text and all the pictures of the submarines could swim around together.

Second mistake: Charlie decided to save everybody some money and proof the job to the client on screen rather than getting **Cromalin** proofs made. Inkjet machines were not good enough to do the job back then, and digital proofs were not yet available.

As we are using CMYK to print this book I cannot actually show you the two RGB colours Charlie picked – but I can show you where he picked them and also how to see them for yourself. If you go into Photoshop and click on the foreground colour chip near the foot of the Tools window, the Colour Picker window appears.

The locations of the two blues are shown in the screen capture of the Colour Picker in figs. **3.3** and **3.4**. In both cases, Charlie selected the area he wanted by clicking on the vertical rainbow-coloured bar in the middle of the window and then clicking in the top right of the big square of colour to its left. This allowed him to choose the exact shade he wanted. The numerical RGB values for the two colours were 0-R, 0-G, 255-B for the darker blue, and 0-R, 255-G, 255-B for the lighter blue.

Then Charlie filled the entire brochure panel with a linear graduated tint of the two shades, starting with the darker blue at the bottom and fading to the lighter blue at the top. It looked great, and he went ahead with placing the text and photographs.

Unfortunately, Charlie had picked two shades of blue that do not actually exist within the CMYK range. By not bothering to run a proof, Charlie was letting the imagesetter convert all

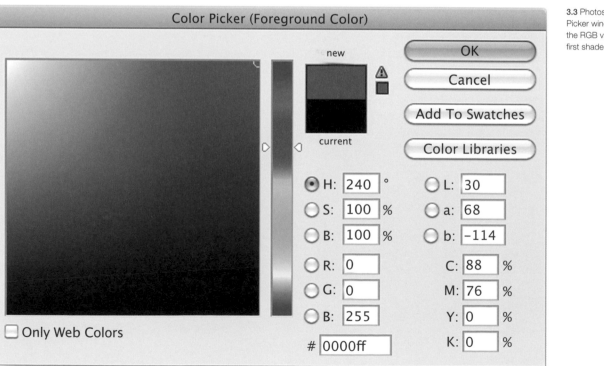

3.3 Photoshop's Colour Picker window showing the RGB values for the first shade of blue…

the RGB colours into CMYK as it produced the film. So, the first time anyone saw the result was when it was coming off the end of a four-colour Heidelberg press at 3,000 copies per hour. It looked awful.

By not running a proof, Charlie did not save any money at all – quite the reverse, in fact – and of course it was the print shop's loss. The other problem was that it was impossible to give the client what he had seen on screen and now really wanted – because the colours could not be created using CMYK. In the end, the print shop lost the job, and Charlie very nearly lost his job as well.

Of course, if he had known what was going to happen in the transition from RGB to CMYK, Charlie could still have started with the RGB colours but then desaturated them a bit (see Chapter 11), which might easily have given him some completely acceptable choices from within the CMYK range.

Look at the CMYK percentages showing in the lower right-hand corner of the darker blue image in fig. 3.3: 88% cyan, 76% magenta. Normally, there should be no problem printing that. But how about if we respecify the colour by entering those

exact percentages in the CMYK area itself, rather than just picking a colour that looks nice? While we do it, watch what happens to the little circle that is currently up in the top right corner of the big colour square on the left.

As we enter the percentages, the circle moves to a completely new position (fig. **3.5**). In addition, the colour shown in the 'this is your new colour' area (i.e. the upper half of the rectangle that appears to the left of the Cancel button; the lower half of it shows the colour currently selected at the time you opened the Colour Picker window) is now displaying the colour indicated by the current position of the little circle in the big square. The small triangular warning sign (which used to be just between the New Colour rectangle and the Cancel button) has also vanished. That was the 'out of gamut' warning. It appears only when you have chosen a colour that is out of the CMYK range.

The little square box that appears under the 'out of gamut' triangle shows you the CMYK colour that is closest to the RGB colour you picked. Of course, you still cannot trust it to show you an accurate CMYK colour, because it is appearing on your

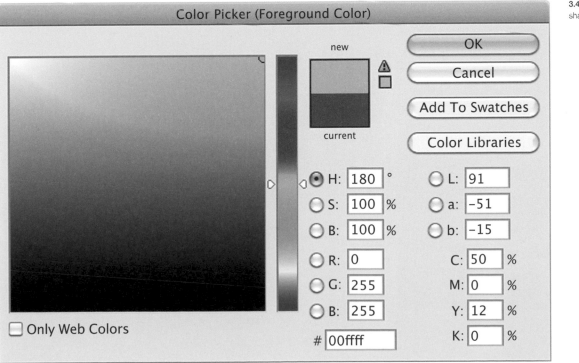

3.4 … and for the second shade of blue

RGB screen. It is also very small, and therefore hard to see properly. But it can be very, very different from the colour you originally picked. If you click on it, it will fill the New Colour area with the same CMYK tint, and then vanish.

It is therefore very important to understand that the big coloured box on the left side of the window is the RGB Colour Picker, and it includes a huge range of colours beyond those available using just the CMYK pigments.

All the major graphics programs allow you to use RGB colours that are likely to be outside the CMYK range. Only comparatively recently (since version 6.5) did Quark replace the RGB red, green and blue swatches offered in the default set with CMYK versions, despite the fact that they should never, ever, be used in documents destined for print. Incidentally, there is no purpose in having CMYK versions of R, G and B in the swatches palettes of either Quark or InDesign. If you want a blue, for example, you will always mix the colour you actually want rather than using the dismal one offered in the default set. And if you do use an RGB colour, the problem will only become apparent when it is too late, unless you run a digital proof before actual film or plate output. Even then it will slow the job down, as changes will have to be made, which may mean a deadline is missed.

There is an old but accurate saying in the print industry: if you catch the problem at the artwork stage, fixing it will cost you roughly the price of a takeout lunch; at the film or plate stage it will cost ten lunches; and if it gets onto the press, a hundred. But nowadays, lunch costs more.

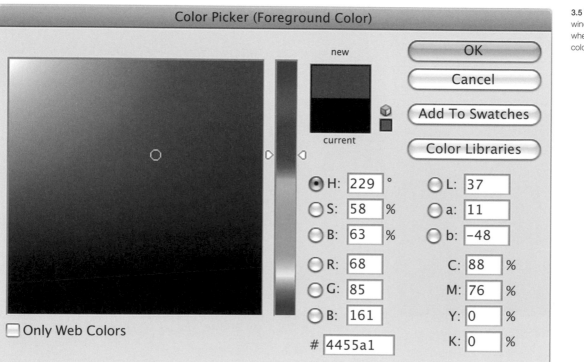

3.5 The Colour Picker window can be misleading when choosing a CMYK colour.

How do You Pick the Colours You Need?

It is difficult. There are useful guides out there, but sometimes it is a bit of a shot in the dark using them. Probably the most common aids to colour selection are the books in the Pantone range or other tint books from a variety of sources.

I deal specifically with Pantone Matching System (PMS) colours in Chapter 10, so I will not say much about them here. However, if you are using the Pantone Process Guide, or the Pantone Solid to Process Guide, or any other kind of tint book, read on.

The Pantone Process Guide is definitely the one to use when you are trying to create CMYK tints for a print job.

To quote Pantone, 'The Pantone Process Guide displays over 3,000 CMYK colour combinations on coated stock. Chromatically arranged for fast colour selection, these guides are an ideal way to visualize, communicate and control applied process colours for type, logos, borders, backgrounds and other graphics treatments.'

All you need to do is select your colour from the book, read what the CMYK tint specification is, enter those values for a new colour in your design software, and use it. And that is all. You do not need to worry about how it looks on screen because you know it will print so close to the colour you picked from the book that nobody will have cause for complaint. Also, as the process guide uses all four CMYK colours it is a much more useful tool than a simple tint book, as you will see.

The Pantone Solid to Process Guide, to quote Pantone again, 'shows what happens when you attempt to reproduce a solid Pantone Matching System colour in four-colour process printing. Although many can be successfully simulated, the majority cannot due to the limitations of the four-colour process as compared to using pre-mixed inks. The fan-guide displays 1,089 solid Pantone colours on coated stock alongside their closest four-colour process match. The CMYK screen values are provided for each colour.'

In other words, do not pick a PMS colour and then expect a CMYK tint to be able to match it, because most likely it cannot.

Tint books can be both a blessing and a curse. As they come from a variety of sources they can range from being very useful (the Pantone Process Guide) to almost useless (lots of the other ones). Some printers produce their own, based on the particular levels at which they like to run CMYK work in-house. Obviously, these are most accurate only when you have sent your work to that particular print shop. Unfortunately, there are lots and lots of print shops out there.

Typically, each of the (quite large) pages in this kind of tint book is divided into many small squares of colour. The

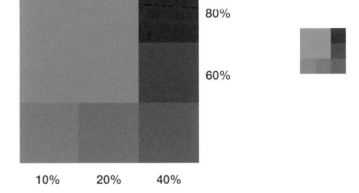

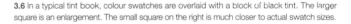

3.6 In a typical tint book, colour swatches are overlaid with a block of black tint. The larger square is an enlargement. The small square on the right is much closer to actual swatch sizes.

row down the left side is a light shade of magenta – 5% or 10%. As you continue across the page, each row increases in density until the very right-hand column is a solid 100%. The same is true of cyan, but this will start with a light tint at the top of the page and gradually increase to a 100% solid on the bottom row. The result is a very light tint in the square at top left and a very dense colour in the square at bottom right. This first page has no yellow whatsoever. On page 2, all the squares are overprinted with a yellow tint of perhaps 5%. On page 3, it is increased to 10%. On page 4, it is 15% – and so on until at the end of the book it is a 100% overlay. So, you have all the possible combinations of cyan, magenta and yellow in increments of 5% or 10% all the way up to 100% of each. Incidentally, try not to select any colour where the combination of the three ink densities adds up to more than 270%, or you will probably run into 'picking' (see Chapter 6).

Unfortunately, most tint books are set up without black appearing, and this can lead to serious problems. For an in-depth description, see 'GCR in Action' in Chapter 6.

When black is involved in a tint book it tends to be in one of two ways. The first is when you get an envelope with the book containing a piece of clear film showing squares containing different strengths of a black tint. The idea is to lay it down over one of the colour swatches in the book to see the combination of the two. Right from the start, the addition of the film clouds the appearance of the colours, and it becomes cloudier and more yellow as it ages.

The second way is when each of the (already quite small) colour swatches in the book has a border along two sides on which a few (even smaller) blocks of black tint are overprinted (fig. **3.6**).

As you can see, the size of the black overprinted areas is so small that it is extremely difficult to tell what the colour really looks like.

Neither of the above methods really works if you wish to select colours that include black. In that event you would be much better off using the Pantone Process Guide.

Some Colour Psychology

What would you say if I asked you to pick a colour to use as a headline in an ad – a colour that could not be ignored, that literally forced people to take notice of it? The chances are you would say 'bright red'. But why? What is so special about red? Why are all our stop lights, danger signals, fire equipment and so on painted red? Even though we probably cannot explain quite why that should be the case, we still somehow recognize that a light green, for example, just would not work the same way.

Here is a possible, and plausible, reason.

Our eyes contain two different kinds of light-sensing cells: rod and cone cells. Rod cells pick up only light intensity and do not transmit any colour information. Cone cells pick up only colour – but they are selective. Some pick up red, some pick up green, and some pick up blue. And they are not all present in the same ratio.

Imagine how things might have been 50,000 years ago, when we were physically just about the same as we are now but had not made any technological advances beyond the use of basic tools. Then consider what the natural environment would have been like. There would not have been many things that looked blue other than the sky and the ocean. The people who lived back then did not – could not – make use of either. There were no boats or planes. So blue was there, but it was not very important in terms of day-to-day survival.

Green, on the other hand, was important. If there was lots of green around, it meant that things were growing, which in turn meant that there was a source of food available, either from the green stuff itself or from other animals that were eating it. So it was very important, but it was not a problem.

How about red? Strangely enough, there are very few things in the natural environment that are red. Sunsets and sunrises, and some flowers and berries – and since many red berries are poisonous, the ability to recognize red was important. But generally, if a lot of red was visible, it usually meant that somebody was wounded or that something was on fire. So red was not only important, it could trigger immediate action in a way no other colour ever did. So it came to mean 'pay attention, right now' and has become particularly associated with urgency and danger.

The ratio between the cone cells, red to green to blue, is 40:20:1. So we have evolved to able to see, recognize and respond to red better than any other colour.

However, if you want to create a headline that is not particularly noticeable at all, try a nice pale blue.

Getting the Most Out of Your Monitor

The first thing to ask yourself is whether you are prepared to spend some money calibrating your monitor, or if you want to try something that is free and may work very well. For the free approach, read on. To spend money, see 'Other Calibration Methods' on page 45.

In order to determine how close your monitor is to telling the truth, you need to have some printed images as well as the actual image files that were used to produce the film and/or plates from which they were printed. However, before using the method described overleaf, or any other calibration method, first run through the following monitor checklist.

1. CRT monitors are pretty rare now. They can be calibrated using either the 'backwards calibration' method, or by one of the software/hardware solutions, both described over the page. So, are you using a good-quality flat-screen monitor? If you are using a low-quality or slightly faulty monitor, this chapter will not be of much help to you.

2. Make sure your monitor is displaying 'Thousands of colours' (i.e. 16-bit) or more.

3. Do you have a background image on your desktop that is visible while you use Photoshop? If so, it will affect your judgement of colour. Best, though boring, would be to replace it with a neutral grey, created using equal R, G and B values of 128. On a scale of 256 shades, 128 represents the halfway point between on and off. If it is applied to all three colours the result is a 50% grey, an ideal background against which you can judge colour and tone.

4. If your monitor has digital controls that allow you to choose the white point, try starting with it set to 6500K.

5. Macs have a transparent workspace that allows you to see the desktop image while working in applications such as Photoshop. This appearance will continually dilute your perception of the colours in the image you are working on. Any neutral, mid-tone grey will be better. This can be put in place by opening the system preferences and choosing Desktop & Screen Saver. Click on Desktop and then choose Solid Colours from the list. There are two grey options available, both of which work well. PCs do not have this problem, as Photoshop, Illustrator and InDesign all use a neutral grey background as a default.

6. Many users will consider all of the above to be important while completely ignoring one of the most important points of all: the lighting in your working environment. You have to control this if you can, otherwise any other calibration you do will be compromised. Lights can be turned on or off; the sun goes up and comes back down again; some days are overcast, some are bright. All these variables affect how everything in your field of vision appears to you, including the images displayed on your monitor. If you are serious about getting things right in print, you will aim to have as few variables as possible getting in the way. Figure out the kind of lighting that will work best for you, and try to stick with it. And never, ever, work with light reflecting off the screen. It is not only bad for colour judgement, it is bad for your eyes.

7. Monitors get old, so you should check and recalibrate if necessary every two or three months. If you find that you can no longer set it the way you used to, and need to, then unfortunately it is time for a new monitor.

Hopefully you already have, or can get hold of, some images that have been placed into a Quark or InDesign file that has then been printed on an offset press. They do not have to be the full-size versions – it is fine to use lower-resolution copies. The best kind of image to work with is either a **TIFF (tagged image file format)** or **PSD (Photoshop document)** file; don't use an **EPS (encapsulated PostScript)** file if you work in Quark, as they don't look great on screen. The important thing is that the colour has not been adjusted at all since the job was printed. You will also need a representative printed copy (from the 'good' part of the run).

Backwards Calibration

Holding the printed copy in your hand, and with the image open in (best) Photoshop or (next best) InDesign (followed by Illustrator, then Quark), adjust the settings on your monitor until the two are as close as you can possibly make them. The more images you can do this with, the better. When in doubt, I open up about ten small images and work on the monitor adjustments while they are all right in front of me. You may find that while most of the colour range is reasonably accurate, one area may be more or less saturated than you are happy with. If so, you will need to estimate roughly how much lighter or darker a particular colour is, and then you can try recalibrating your monitor.

With any calibration method there is usually a degree of compromise, but that is all we can really hope for. It is just not possible to completely rely on your monitor for accurate colour. Fortunately, the kind of mix in a typical continuous-tone image means it is slightly less susceptible to variations in appearance than an area of flat colour, where a slight difference can radically affect the result. Fortunately, the flat areas are the easy ones to fix. Therefore, while not being able to completely trust what you see on screen, you can at least calibrate things to the point of being able to trust the mid-tone information that your monitor is showing you, and possibly much more. You cannot use it to visually judge the highlights, or the shadows, and especially not the exact colours – but for the general appearance, and the overall lightness or darkness of the mid-tone range, you can open up an image on screen and know that it is extremely close to how the printed result will look.

I have used backwards calibration to get amazingly accurate colour output from the print shop without having to trust my monitor 100%. To do the same, you will need a good tint book and a good desktop inkjet printer, or some other way of producing colour prints of your work.

If you do not have a reasonably modern inkjet printer – and by reasonably modern I mean one that can produce images at a resolution of at least 720dpi and preferably much higher – then you are missing out on a very useful piece of equipment (see Chapter 7 for more about inkjet resolution). These printers are amazingly cheap, especially in A4 (UK) or letter size (US) formats, and their high-resolution prints, when they are on the right paper, are superb.

The manufacturers of inkjet printers tend to sell them at very slightly more than cost, making them look like an extremely reasonable purchase. Then they truly stick it to you for the ink. I am reliably informed that, weight for weight, inkjet ink is more expensive than gold.

The idea is that you can use the inkjet printer to generate a print you are happy with, then use the tint book and the print to figure out what colour specifications you actually need in the image on screen.

For this example, let us say you have designed a book cover. It is all there on your monitor, and it looks great. Then you print it out and you are not quite so happy. So you have to adjust the colour and continue to print it out until you have a print of a book cover you will be proud to include in your portfolio. This is the one you are going to show the client as a final design draft.

In order to use a tint book as an aid to the following, you need a good tint book rather than one that shows only colours made up from C, M and Y – such as many produced by print shops. Instead, try to obtain a copy of the Pantone Process Colour Guide (see Chapter 10), which includes tints made from *all* the CMYK colours.

Print out another copy and cut little holes in it so that you can put it down over the pages in the tint book. Move it around until you find the square that is the closest colour match to it, then adjust the tint specifications in the software until they match those shown in the tint book.

This is easy to do when creating images in Adobe Illustrator or CorelDRAW, where you have to decide what colour to make everything anyway. It is much harder to achieve using Adobe Photoshop, where you are very often working with continuous-tone images. However, with practice, it can be done – especially if your design allows you to make selections of certain areas and adjust them without disturbing things in the rest of the image. Use the individual channel settings in the Levels and/or Curves windows after placing markers on the image with the Colour Picker tool. Then, the Info window can give you before/after information as you make adjustments. If you have previously calibrated your monitor using the method described below, you should easily be able to tell if your image is getting out of hand.

As for the areas that backwards calibration cannot reach – the highlights and shadows – these can be calibrated very accurately using the method described in the next chapter.

Other Calibration Methods

Beginning with CS4, Adobe discontinued including Adobe Gamma calibration software for PCs, as it was primarily a means of calibrating CRT monitors. They have therefore moved away from an 'eyes only' approach and left... nothing in its place, although, oddly enough, the Display Calibrator Assistant (fig. **3.7**) is still available on the Mac platform. This is not an Adobe product, however, and is not designed to address calibration issues regarding print output.

If you are prepared to spend some money on calibration rather than using the 'backwards calibration' method already described, and/or if your monitor does not come with any way to adjust light and colour levels, try one of the following alternatives, which deal with calibration in a way suitable for all types of display, regardless of your monitor type.

i1Display 2 from X-rite
http://www.xrite.com/product_overview.aspx?ID=788

baslCColour print
http://www.basiccolor.de/english/Product%20Overview%20 Q2-2007.pdf (page 8)

Spyder3Elite
http://www.datacolor.eu/en/products/monitor-calibration/ spyder3elite/index.html

All these offer excellent solutions for achieving accurate calibration, and the last mentioned has received numerous awards from magazines including *Macworld*, *iDIGITAL*, *PCPhoto*, *Personal Computer World* and *DigitalPHOTO*. While it is possible that even after using one of these you will still have to manually adjust monitor settings to match the results you are getting from the print shop, it is much less likely.

3.7 The Display Calibrator Assistant is available on the Mac platform and can be used to help calibrate monitors.

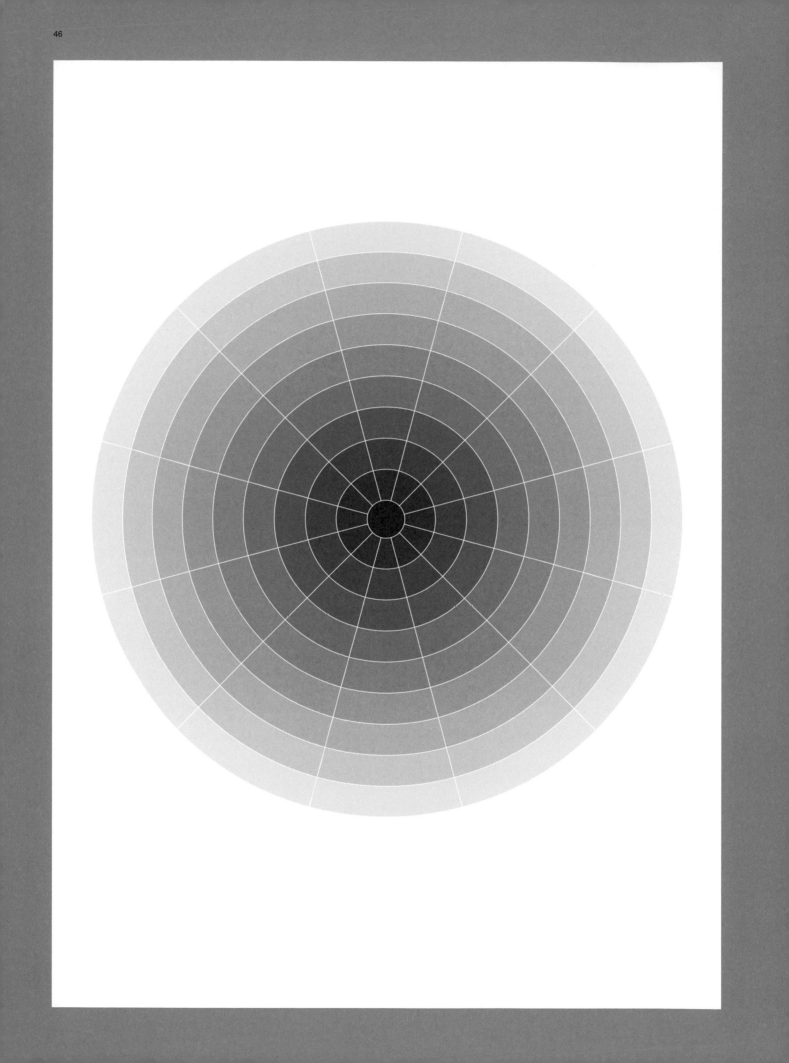

Calibrating a Greyscale Image

4

As well as the problems presented by converting RGB to CMYK, the actual printing process itself has some additional surprises in store. 'Dot gain', the bane of designers everywhere, is rarely understood and therefore not usually taken into account. Adobe Photoshop, InDesign, Illustrator and Acrobat can remove some of the sting from its inky tail by tagging work with a digital 'colour management system' (CMS), but unless the correct CMS is put into place the result will be second best (see Chapter 6). But even Photoshop will not help with calibrating shadows and highlights: those are areas you have to deal with yourself.

While this may become automated in the future, it has not happened yet. Dot gain means that what you see on your screen is not what will print on an offset press, even if you are looking at a black-and-white photo. Big dots get bigger, and small dots get smaller. And only you can fix it.

Opposite: Halftone dots are tricky customers. Highlights and shadows require careful treatment if they are to survive.

Dealing with Highlights and Shadows

Here is a very simple method that takes all the worry out of trying to set image highlights and shadows properly. With a little experience, you will confidently be able to handle this kind of calibration in any kind of image without relying on anyone's help.

But first, why do you need to be particularly concerned with the highlights and shadows? The answer lies in understanding the nature of the offset printing process. While you are working on a digital file, everything is perfect – as far as transfer of the data is concerned. You could copy the file back and forth from one system to another again and again, and as long as nothing actually went wrong, you would end up with exactly the same file that you started with. However, once you get out into the 'real' world, it is a different matter. Imagine making a copy of a videotape. Then a copy of the copy. Then a copy of the copy of the copy, and so on. Pretty soon, there would be no video any more, just garbage. Each time you make a non-digital transfer, you lose a percentage of the quality of the original, and the problem is compounded with each subsequent transfer. When you send your file off to the printer, the process that gets the file onto the press is most likely digital; therefore there is no loss of data. However, the transfer of the inked image from the plate to the blanket is a physical transfer, which therefore involves some data loss. But the biggest change in the data occurs when the blanket transfers the image to the paper. That is because, as well as being a physical transfer, paper tends to allow ink to absorb into it and spread along the fibres from which it is made. Obviously, some papers – newsprint, for example – will do this a lot, whereas others, such as coated papers, hardly do it at all.

The result of this is generally referred to as 'dot gain'. To be really accurate, dot gain actually refers to the increase in density of a 50% dot on a piece of film compared to the resulting density when it is finally printed on the paper. However, in terms of effect on the image, it is not only the mid-tones that undergo change; in the shadow areas, the big dots also get bigger, and in the highlights, the small dots get smaller.

The effect of this on the appearance of the highlights and shadows is very detrimental. If you started with an image where the tone range ran all the way from black through to white, after it had been printed the tone within many of the highlights and shadows simply would not exist any more. Highlights would have burned out to white, while shadows would have filled in to black. Typically this means that your image now has holes in the sky and holes in the ground.

It may be obvious or it may be quite subtle. It may be quite difficult, looking at the result, to pin down exactly why it looks wrong. But instinctively, you know that something is not quite right with the picture, and your natural tendency is to leave it behind and go on to something else – the next article, picture, whatever. Mentally, you turn your back on it. Which, if the image is part of an advertisement, intended to make you buy something, is a marketing disaster.

Remember, all you need to be is convincing – and holes in the sky or the ground are not convincing.

You do not need to worry about the mid-tones yet. If you have calibrated your workflow using the method described in the previous chapter, the mid-tones can be fixed along the way as you deal with the highlights and shadows.

What you have to do is squeeze the entire tonal range slightly and thus artificially flatten the contrast. By deliberately flattening the contrast in the image, you are making the smallest dots slightly larger, and the largest dots slightly smaller. During the printing process, all will undergo dot gain, thus getting respectively smaller and larger but without burning out or filling in. The amount by which you need to do this primarily depends on the kind of paper you intend to print on. Is it a high-quality coated paper or newsprint? Will the ink stay more or less in place, or will it spread out along the fibres of the paper as soon as it touches it? If you are printing on a coated paper, allow a 3% to 5% buffer zone at either end. For uncoated paper it is likely to be between 8% and 12%. For newsprint, it starts at around 12% but can be as much as 20%. These are approximate dot-gain values for sheet-fed printing. Web-offset values can be considerably higher.

Creating a Dot-gain Test Strip

Dot gain also depends on the quality of the printing machine and the person running it. Try asking the printers at what point – i.e. at what percentage – the shadow dots will fill in and the highlight dots burn out, given the paper you have chosen and the press they plan to run the job on. If you are lucky, the printers will already have a pretty good idea of what will happen, and might even have run some tests of their own.

If not, and you plan on using the printers for a lot of your work, suggest that it might be to their advantage in the long run if they do some calibration tests for you. You will need to supply them with a dot-gain test strip, which you can easily make as a simple AI (Adobe Illustrator), TIFF or EPS file. To create one of these, draw a series of twenty-one small squares, something like the example shown (fig. **4.1**). You can create these in many applications, but if you use (for example) Illustrator you can turn off any colour management so that the tint values are not changed. To do this, choose Edit > Assign Profile > Don't Colour Manage this Document. You can then open the result in Photoshop and check that the grey percentages have not changed. If you get some of the colour-management options appearing as you open the file, check the notes at the end of Chapter 6 to help you decide what to do. (Do not miss these – they could be very important!) Fill the central box with a 50% grey. For the ten boxes to the left, fill the first with a 1% tint, the second with a 2% tint, and so on up to 10%. For the right-hand boxes, start at 90% and go all the way up to 99%.

Ask the printers to position it outside the live area on a print job running the same paper stock that you plan to use (or something very similar, if that is not possible) and on the same press. If you plan to use the printers a lot, suggest that they run it on as many variations of paper and press as they can for a while. Soon you will have a very accurate picture of what will happen on different presses using a wide range of papers. Ask the printers to check the 50% value of each sample with a **densitometer**. The difference between the original 50% tint and the value shown by the densitometer is the dot-gain factor, which can then be compensated for using the colour-management settings (see Chapter 6).

In a good printed halftone, the density never becomes completely filled in, or burned out. There should be a very, very light speckling of dots of white in the darkest areas, and of black in the lightest. So, if there is a medium to high percentage of burn-out in one of the squares, you should adjust to the next higher value for the highlights and the next lower value for the shadows. If, for example, lots of the 4% highlight dots did not make it, but only a few of the 5% dots vanished, you will

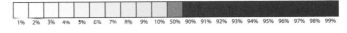

4.1 A calibration strip that, when printed, will tell you where the highlight and shadow dots burn out or fill in, as well as giving you a dot-gain factor for a 50% tint.

have to adjust the tone range to allow for a 4% loss at that end of the scale. Therefore the lightest tint in the image after calibration will be 5%. If, at the other end of the spectrum, lots of the tiny white dots still show in the 93% square but the 94% square is almost completely filled in to black, you will have to adjust for a 7% loss at that end, and therefore the darkest pixels that should be left in your image will be 93%.

This will take care of the highlights and shadows beautifully.

A Practical Example
of Greyscale Calibration

Open the image you want to calibrate in Adobe Photoshop (fig. **4.2** shows my example).

The first thing to do is to open the Levels window (Image > Adjustments > Levels) in order to make a basic adjustment to the tonal range so that it extends from black to white (see fig. **4.3**).

The Input histogram, in the centre of the window, shows the 'pixel pile' – i.e. which shades of grey are present in the image, and the relative quantity of each one. Think of it as being made up of 256 vertical columns, one for each shade, beginning with black on the far left and ending with white on the far right, and that each column is filled proportionally according to the number of pixels there are of that particular colour.

A gap at one or both ends indicates that the tonal range doesn't extend right out to black or white, so the first thing to do for *most* images is to stretch the entire pixel pile out so that it does.

To reset the black point, drag the small arrow situated on the left-hand end of the histogram so that it just touches the pixel pile on the left-hand end. Histograms often end in small tails that indicate that there are just a few pixels of those shades present. Keeping them may be a good idea, or not. The only way to tell is to zoom in on some of the darkest or lightest areas and keep an eye on what happens when you move the arrow back and forth across the tail. If it doesn't make much difference, it is probably okay to cut the tail off, just where the pile begins to pick up. Then do the same with the white point arrow to the right of the histogram, as shown in fig. **4.4**. Cutting the tail off here means deleting subtle data in the highlights of the image.

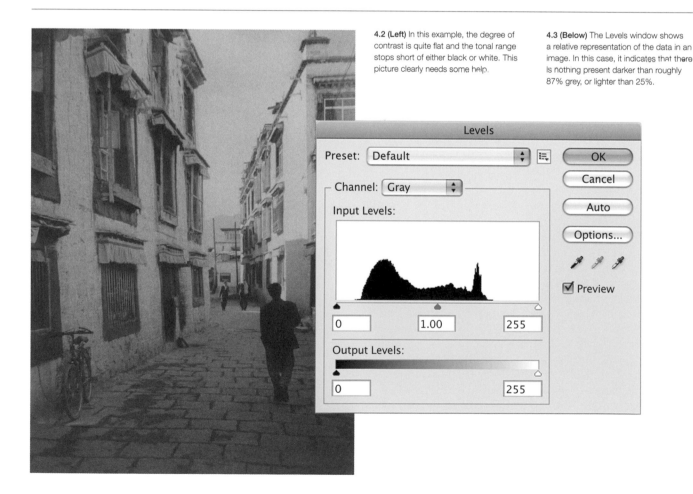

4.2 (Left) In this example, the degree of contrast is quite flat and the tonal range stops short of either black or white. This picture clearly needs some help.

4.3 (Below) The Levels window shows a relative representation of the data in an image. In this case, it indicates that there is nothing present darker than roughly 87% grey, or lighter than 25%.

Sometimes you will want to keep these in place, but usually they are not very important.

You will probably have noticed that I have made no mention, so far, of any adjustment involving the middle arrow. That is because, in almost every case, it should only be moved after the black and white points have been set. Then, if the mid-tones look too dark, move the arrow slightly to the left. This puts more of the pixel pile to its right, i.e. on the lighter side of the range. To darken the mid-tones, move it to the right. Rather than moving it in tiny increments, I usually give it a good heave one way or the other – thus overdoing the adjustment – then bring it slowly back towards the centre. Doing this is far more likely to result in a better adjustment. The image now looks as shown in fig. **4.5**.

Click OK and then reopen the Levels window. The pile will now extend right across the histogram area, but there will probably be vertical grey lines through it. These are shades that don't exist in the image: we began this process with a finite number, and we still have a finite number, which have been redistributed, causing gaps. Fortunately, the gaps are evenly spaced throughout the pixel pile, so it is not a problem. Most **greyscale** images still appear convincing even when made from as few as 75 shades. For example, fig. 4.20 shows two apparently identical sections of the image. One of them shows the same number of shades as the original image, distributed evenly between 5% and 95%. Next to it is a copy in which the number of shades of grey has been restricted to 75 – also distributed evenly between 5% and 95%. Can you tell which one is the restricted sample?

4.4 (Below) The Levels window showing how to reposition the black and white points.

4.5 (Right) This adjustment spreads the tone in the image from black to white.

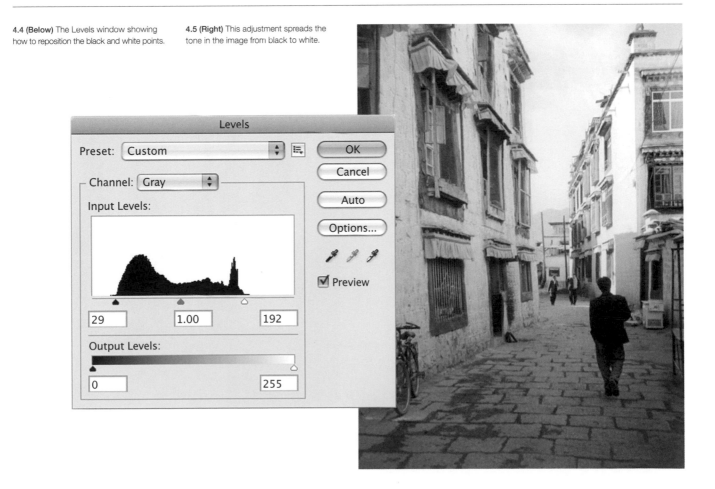

Now close the Levels window again. As it is just about impossible to accurately identify the darkest and lightest parts of an image, we need to use Photoshop to help us do so. Before starting this process, open the Info window (fig. **4.6**) and check to make sure that it is showing greyscale information ('K' values) in the top left quarter. If not, click on the Options button, select Palette Options and set the first colour readout to Actual Colour. Then, open the Threshold window by choosing Image > Adjustments > Threshold (fig. **4.7**). The image will immediately change, becoming black and white (fig. **4.8**).

The same histogram shape appears, but with only one adjustment arrow. The mid-point position of the arrow (the threshold) indicates that all the areas in the image showing as black are to the left of the arrow and therefore darker than a

50% grey, whereas areas showing in white are to the right of the arrow and therefore lighter than 50%. The default position of the arrow when you open the Threshold window is at 128, which is the mid-point of a 256-shade greyscale image.

Move the arrow towards the left-hand end of the pixel pile (fig. **4.9**). Gradually, the black areas in the image shrink (fig. **4.10**). The further you move the arrow, the fewer areas are left that are darker than the threshold level. When you are close to the left-hand end of the pixel pile, only the very darkest areas in the image are left showing.

Take a good look – so that you can remember where they are – and then click Cancel.

Choose the Colour Sampler tool, which is the second tool down in the Eyedropper tool flyout (fig. **4.11**). Clicking on the

---

4.6 The Info window, showing 'K' values in the top left quarter.

4.7 (Inset) The Threshold window at its default position of 128.
4.8 The resulting change in the appearance of the image. Anything lighter than 50% grey shows as white, while darker values show as black.

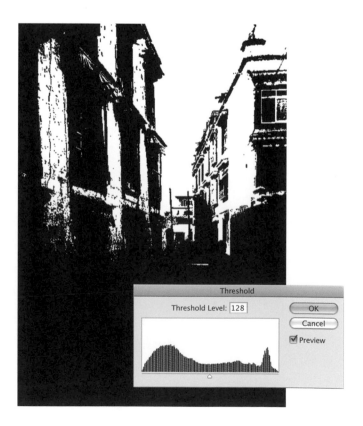

image with this tool places up to four markers. These appear in the Info window, telling you the exact percentage of grey of the pixel directly beneath each one. Better still, as you make adjustments to the image, they will give you live 'before' and 'after' information, showing you how the percentages are changing. The idea is to place one marker on the darkest pixel you can find, and another on the lightest, and then adjust the image until both are showing the percentages that you want.

Now you know roughly where to place your first marker, zoom in and move the cursor around in that area, and, as you do so, watch the numbers change in the 'K' area of the Info window. Find the darkest pixel you can, and then click on it. You will see the area for marker 1 appear in the Info window, showing the exact shade of grey clicked on.

Incidentally, markers can be dragged to new positions, or deleted by holding down the Alt key and clicking on them. Once I have accurately positioned them, I usually leave them in place in case I need to calibrate the image for a different process in the future. They do not interfere with printing and can only be seen when the image is open in Photoshop.

Then repeat the process, but move the Threshold arrow to the right (fig. **4.12**). This time, the last areas left visible indicate the lightest pixels in the image (fig. **4.13**). As before, click Cancel and place a second marker on the lightest pixel you can find. Both markers should now be visible (fig. **4.14**), and the Info window should now look something like fig. **4.15**.

Now for the actual calibration. In order to create a 5% 'gap' at either end of the scale, we need to pull the information

4.9 (Inset) The Threshold arrow is pulled to the left of the pixel pile.
4.10 Only the darkest areas of the image are still able to appear.

4.11 The Colour Sampler tool.

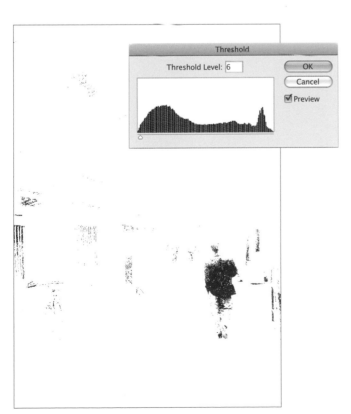

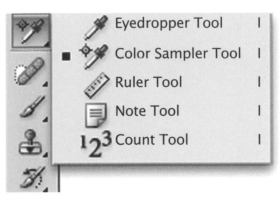

in the image further out towards solid black and white, to leave the darkest point set at 95% and the brightest at 5%.

 If you had not made the initial Levels adjustment, the pixel pile might stop short of either end of the scale. In this case, the adjustment can be made simply by pulling the black and/or white arrows (situated just below the histogram, at either end) in towards the pixel pile.

 However, if you have made the kind of adjustment described previously the information *will* extend out to both ends of the scale. Also, by having done so, you will have created slightly greater contrast between each pair of shades, and this should make it easier to find and click on the darkest/lightest pixels. In order to make the necessary adjustment, you should drag the arrows situated at either end of the

Output Levels arrow (that is, the area under the histogram filled with a graduated grey tint) until the Info window tells you that the correct percentage of adjustment has been made at both ends of the scale. These arrows can be used to 'squash' the entire histogram from one or both ends without cutting off any of the pixel information. Alternatively, you could make the adjustment using the numerical Output Levels boxes. The histogram represents 256 shades of grey; therefore, a 1% change equals 2.56 shades. A 5% change would be 12.8 shades, but as we can adjust only in whole numbers, the closest we can get is 13. Therefore you would change the 0 to 13 and the 255 to 242. In this example, the Info and Levels window now look as shown in figs **4.16** and **4.17**.

4.12 (Inset) The Threshold arrow is pulled to the right of the pixel pile.
4.13 Only the lightest areas of the image are still able to appear.

4.14 The image, showing both markers in place.
4.15 (Inset) The Info window showing 'before' and 'after' marker information prior to any calibration adjustment.

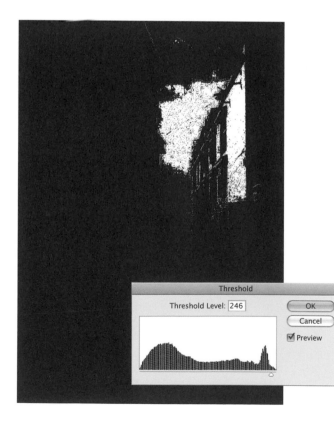

If you click OK to accept these changes, the calibration of the image – at least as far as the highlights and shadows are concerned – is complete. The Levels window will now show a gap representing 5% at both ends of the histogram (fig. **4.18**), and the image will print as shown in fig. **4.19**.

And that is basically it.

The white gaps now showing between the vertical black lines in the Levels histogram are just that: shades that are not represented in your image. Unless these gaps are wide, it is very unlikely to be a problem, as we can get away with far fewer shades of grey than you might think, and still be convincing. For example, fig. **4.20** shows two apparently identical sections of the image. One of them shows the same number of shades as the original image, distributed evenly between 5% and 95%.

Next to it is a copy in which the number of shades of grey has been restricted to 75 – also distributed evenly between 5% and 95%. Can you tell which one is which?

Remember – each image is different and you should not make the same blind adjustment to everything. An image may, for example, include specular highlights such as reflections on a chrome bumper, or lights in a night scene. These should be completely white, and will not look right if you have filled them with a 5% highlight dot. Similarly, a photograph of a foggy scene is unlikely to contain very dense shadow tones. These will look much too dark if you pull them back out to a value of 95% black.

4.16 and 4.17 (Below) The Info window updates as changes are made to the black and white point arrows in the Output Levels field. In this example, the new shadow value is 95% and the new highlight value is 5%. **4.18 (Bottom)** The new spread of tone values in the calibrated image. The vertical white gaps represent shades of grey that are no longer present.

4.19 (Left) The final image after calibration.
4.20 (Right) The one on the far right has 75 shades.

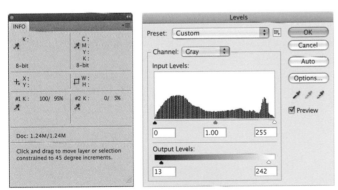

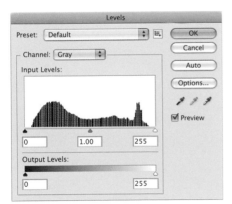

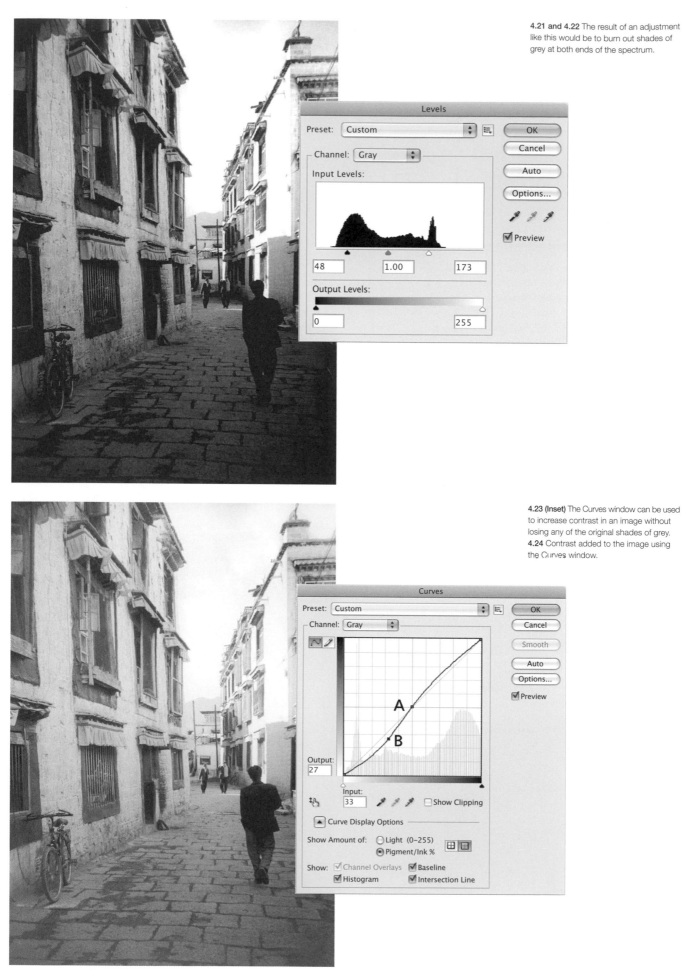

4.21 and 4.22 The result of an adjustment like this would be to burn out shades of grey at both ends of the spectrum.

4.23 (Inset) The Curves window can be used to increase contrast in an image without losing any of the original shades of grey.
4.24 Contrast added to the image using the Curves window.

Adding Contrast

If you decide that, despite your calibration of all the highlights and shadows, the image still needs a bit of extra punch, you may want to add more contrast. Try to avoid using Image > Adjustments > Brightness and Contrast. In fact, it is better if you forget that particular tool completely, as it has a tendency to burn out what were previously light greys to white, and fill in dark greys to black. This is not, as you may think, what you do when you **posterize** an image. Posterizing is where you restrict the image to displaying a particular number of shades of grey. That is different – and very effective, although easily overused. The brightness and contrast adjustments will do that only at the top and bottom of the tonal range – which does produce more contrast, but at the expense of the shades shown in those areas. Once you have wiped out those areas of information, you might never get them back.

Here is an example to show you what I mean.

Let us take the calibrated image and use the Levels window to apply the same kind of adjustment that Brightness and Contrast might give you.

As you can see in fig. **4.21**, I have pulled the black and white arrows in so that they are underneath the pixel information. What this means is that the parts of the histogram that are outside those arrows no longer hold shades of grey. Instead, everything to the right of the white arrow is now white, and everything to the left of the black arrow is now black. The result in the image (fig. **4.22**) would be a much greater degree of contrast – but it is at the expense of all those shades of grey that were left outside when the arrows were moved. If I had also pulled the 50% arrow to the left, I would have added brightness as well.

If you want to add contrast intelligently, what you really need is the Curves window, found under Image > Adjustments > Curves. Once it is open, this is what you do.

Click on the diagonal line at the centre point. This places an 'anchor' (A), with which you can pull the line out towards either the top left or bottom right corners of the window, into a convex or concave curve. This is just like moving the mid-point arrow in the Levels window: pull it one way, and the mid-tones get darker. Pull it the other, and they get lighter. If you need to lighten or darken the mid-tones, go ahead and pull – but otherwise, all you need is an anchor point on the line. If you decide that you do not want a particular anchor point, just click on it and drag it off the square. Click again halfway between your centre point and the bottom left end of the line (B), and pull slightly down and to the right. This pulls the whole line into a slight 'S' curve as it rotates around the anchor point (fig. **4.23**).

By doing this, you pull all the lighter-than-50% tones into a new configuration that makes them brighter in the upper-mid range; at the same time, you push the darker-than-50% tones, making them darker in the lower-mid range. The overall effect is to add brightness and contrast to the image without burning out a single one of the highlight and shadow tones in the original. However, if you pull too hard, you will flat-line the tone range at one or both ends of the spectrum, and that is when the information burns out.

The result of adding contrast in this way, as opposed to that shown in fig. 4.21, can be seen here in fig. **4.24**.

So, now you can adjust the mid-tones through backwards calibration of your monitor (see Chapter 3), and trust them; and calibrate the highlights and shadows within an image, and trust them. So you are well on the way to never again waking up at 3 a.m. worrying about how your greyscale images are going to look!

Bitmaps and Pixel Depth

5

You probably already know what a bitmap is... or do you? Is a JPEG a bitmap? How about a TIFF? And if they are, what about that other, 'one-colour' format you can find in Adobe Photoshop, i.e. 'bitmap'? What does the word 'bitmap' actually mean? What is pixel depth and why should it concern you? Is it something that is important, or is it just background information that does not really matter?

Pixel depth is an important issue that governs not only how many colours an image can contain, but also many of the uses to which it can then be put. For instance, it is a big part of what makes an image suitable only for the web, or only for print. Aside from that, a knowledge of pixel depth can sometimes allow you to fix certain image problems that otherwise cannot be resolved.

Opposite: Using bit-depth to restrict the number of colours in an image can have very creative results.

Why are there 256 Shades in a Greyscale Image?

In the previous chapter, the number 256 was mentioned in relation to the maximum number of shades that (most! see note below) greyscale images in Photoshop can display. So why is it 256 and not 100? Surely we measure tint density as a percentage? While that is generally true, the ways in which digital graphic images are produced has opened things up somewhat.

For instance, we now use an entirely different approach in the actual construction of images. Previously, the use of a screen, positioned between film and the image projected onto it, led to the production of a conventional halftone: a grid of round dots of different sizes, but all of the same colour. Seen from a distance, we do not see the dots. Instead, we see the visual mix of the dots plus the paper showing through between them, as various shades (see Chapter 1). Pure illusion, but it works.

On the computer, the illusion is different. Images are displayed as solid masses of pixels, each one a small square, and there is no space between them at all. In a single image they are all the same size and they can display many different colours. Just how many colours they can display depends on their **bit depth**, i.e. the amount of digital space they occupy on your computer.

To confuse the issue further, your monitor displays these pixels on a grid of its own resolution, typically 96 pixels to the linear inch. This means that the often-quoted resolution of '72dpi' for images destined for the internet is now out of date; if you save an image at a particular size for a website at that resolution, the result will display smaller than you thought, as its pixels will be redistributed at 96 to the inch instead of the anticipated 72.

The simplest kind of image we can display is called a 'bitmap' in Photoshop and is made up of just two colours. In fact, the word 'bitmapped' can refer to any image made up of pixels, and this is one of many instances in which common terminology can easily lead to confusion. For example, we generally think of a dot as round, and yet when we talk about pixels – which are square, of course – we refer to their density in terms of 'dots per inch'. Then, when we are talking about the round dots that end up on the film, the plate, the blanket and eventually the paper, we are much less likely to refer to them as dots and more likely to talk about them collectively as a 'line screen', referring to the number of lines of dots there are to the inch. Small surprise, then, that there is some confusion out there. Let us not even think about the kind of dots you get out of an inkjet printer – yet.

Getting back to our simple bitmap, although the two colours can be any two colours, at their most basic level the pixels are either in a state of being completely 'on', in which case they are white, or completely 'off', in which case they are black. These pixels are called '1-bit deep', and as such they can display just these two states, each of which creates the appropriate colour.

The next level up is 8-bit. Now, there is no reason why we could not have 2-bit, 3-bit, 4-bit and so on – but why bother? For example, if we had a 2-bit image, it could display 2 x 2 states: in other words, four shades of grey. So we would have 0%, 33%, 67% and 100%, which is not especially useful. Instead, the next logical step is for an image that can display enough shades between black and white to produce a really good image; hence 8-bit (which in fact provides rather more shades than are really necessary).

Each of the 8 bits contributes two states to the equation. It is a multiplier, so there are 2 x 2 x 2 x 2 x 2 x 2 x 2 x 2 potential states available for the colour display of each pixel – and that is why there are 256 shades of grey in an 8-bits deep Photoshop greyscale image. It is also possible to specify 16- or even 32-bits of depth, resulting in far more shades – but in almost every case it is not necessary and even 256 shades is more than we really need.

NB If we want to display fewer shades, we can use the Posterize command and pick any number between 2 and 256. A full-colour example and the same image posterized down to just four colours are shown in fig. 5.1, together with the Posterize window.

Pixel Depth
in Colour Images

The next step up in image complexity is colour. There are several different formats of colour image (fig. **5.2**), and the number of colours they can display depends either on how many channels they comprise or whether they are indexed colour, i.e. **GIF (graphics interchange format)**.

GIF images have no place in the printing industry and are strictly for on-screen viewing such as on websites. Indexed colour can show a maximum of 256 colours, which can come from anywhere in the entire RGB range, rather than having to be shades of the same hue. If the colours are **dithered**, i.e. pixels of one colour are scattered throughout a patch of another colour, they visually merge to create the appearance of a colour that is not actually present as one of the 256. Because of this ability, they can appear to be very convincing 'full-colour' continuous-tone images on screen. So convincing, in fact, that you cannot tell just by looking at your monitor whether the image is GIF, **JPEG**, TIFF or EPS format, or whether it is seriously compromised in terms of potential print quality.

If you do have to use a GIF image, it needs to be converted into an acceptable format before it can be printed, and even then it is probably not going to be great because of having been constrained to 256 colours. However, occasionally there are ways to get there (see Chapter 7 for some suggestions on how to turn a GIF or lower-quality JPEG image into something that will print as a convincing colour image).

In a 24-bit RGB colour image (which is the most common format produced by desktop scanners and digital cameras) there are three separate 'channels', each one holding an 8-bit image. (A channel is the part of an image that holds all the information for any one of the component colours.) When they are displayed simultaneously, the colour each one contains becomes transparent, thus allowing all their overlapping colour combinations to be seen. (They can also be looked at individually, in which case it is usually more useful to view them as greyscale images, especially if you are considering changing an RGB image into greyscale format – see 'Useful greyscale options' in Chapter 11.) Thus the three channels together are potentially able to display all the resulting colour combinations. This means that each pixel can display a mix combining any one of the 256 shades of red, plus any one of the 256 shades of green, plus any one of the 256 shades of blue – in other words, any one of 16,777,216 colours.

Now consider what the addition of yet another channel does to this number, since in a CMYK image yet another greyscale map is added. Thus, our 16.7 million is multiplied again by 256, giving us a potential range of 4,294,967,200

colours. This is clearly more colours than we can ever distinguish between. Even the most accomplished painter who spends a lot of time considering colour might only be able to distinguish 20–30,000 of them. However, even though our computers offer us more colours than we can ever distinguish between, it is not a problem – just think of it as an advantage that we cannot actually use.

Someone once tried to sell me a scanner based on its ability to produce 48-bit CMYK images – lovely, no doubt, but pointless. That is 12 bits per channel. Even in an RGB image, a channel depth of 12 bits would allow each pixel in a single channel to display any one of 2 x 2 x 2 x 2 x 2 x 2 x 2 x 2 x 2 x 2 x 2 x 2, or 4,096 colours. Multiply that by itself three times (because it is a three-channel image) and you have nearly 69 billion colours, which is pretty silly. In CMYK it is even sillier: 281 thousand billion.

The important information about any scanner is much more likely to be contained in the answer to the following question: what is its optical scanning resolution? At what resolution can it scan before it starts **interpolating** the image resolution, i.e. spreading the same information over a progressively larger and larger number of pixels? The optical resolution is what will allow you to pick up detail that will otherwise get left behind, so it is extremely important – much more important than having oodles of colours that you cannot even distinguish between. Decent optical resolution starts at around 1200dpi for 'reflective' art, where the light reflects off the object and bounces back to the sensor, and 2400 or (much better) 3600dpi for transparencies, where the light passes through the object to the sensor. The reason for the difference between these is that reflective art such as a print is usually much bigger than a transparency, which can be as small as a 35mm slide. These days, even a fairly cheap scanner is capable of producing an RGB image from reflective art that can be turned into a decent CMYK image.

Given that the range of colour in RGB is larger than in that of CMYK, it is perhaps surprising that a CMYK image can hold a greater number of colours than the same image in RGB. This is due to confusing the range of colours within the two colour spaces with the mathematical limitations imposed on digital images of both types.

The key factor here is that the number of colours potentially available in either format depends only upon the number of colour channels in the image and the bit depth of those channels. If we compare a CMYK image with four 8-bit channels with an RGB image with only three 8-bit channels, clearly the CMYK image must have the potential to display more colours. That

5.2 This image has been divided into different bit depths and formats. From left to right: bitmap (1-bit deep), greyscale (8-bits deep), duotone (16-bits deep, i.e. two 8-bit channels) and CMYK (36-bits deep).

potential is a purely physical limitation imposed by the way the software deals with things. It has nothing whatsoever to do with how many colours actually exist in either system – which, perhaps confusing the issue slightly further, is infinite in both cases: but only because in theory there is no limit to the number of shades you can divide a colour into. In practice, the range is larger in RGB. RGB contains almost every CMYK colour, but CMYK does not come even close to containing every RGB colour. If it did, there would be nothing to discuss – and many fewer problems!

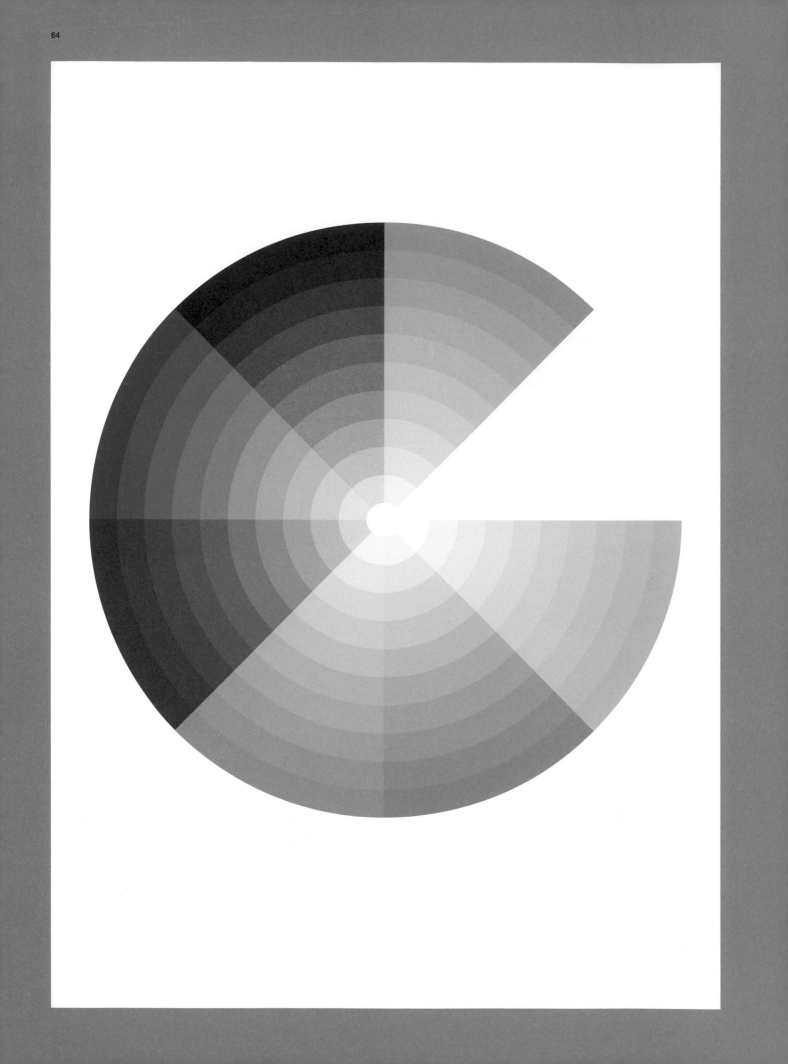

Calibrating Colour Images

If you are working with photos from a variety of sources you will find that they have very different characteristics: some may appear warm, others much cooler. Daylight produces different colour casts depending upon the time of day the shot was taken, and indoor photos will often be lit by a combination of artificial and natural light. Artificial lighting may be fluorescent (cool) or incandescent (warm). All of these present potential problems to the designer, because they add image-wide colour casts which are not wanted.

It is tempting to ask the printer to take care of all this for you, but that is a very costly way to fix something that you could quite easily do yourself. With experience, you will never have to ask someone else to step in and do the work for you – because you can do it better. And, you have the best incentive: nobody else will ever be as concerned about the quality of your work as you are.

As long as you save your work under a new name you do not need to worry about damaging the source material. Add to that the 'history' (the multiple undo capability in Adobe Photoshop), and you can see the process is foolproof: you can always go back to the beginning if you think your adjustments are not good enough. So, jump right in with confidence. Who knows – this may become the part of your design work that you enjoy the most.

Opposite: Too much red, and not enough blue. How do you fix it? What do you do?

Getting Started

We have already covered two of the most important calibration methods: backwards calibration for the mid-tones (see Chapter 3) and greyscale calibration for the highlights and shadows (see Chapter 4).

When faced with trying to calibrate a colour image, you may be tempted to let someone else take care of it. Do not be put off. If you can calibrate greyscale, you can definitely calibrate colour, especially if you have a reasonably good monitor and a tint book. If you need a tint book, talk to a few print shops. If they get the idea that you are a busy graphic designer looking for a reliable printer, they will try to be very helpful. Good print shops update their Pantone references every so often and might have one or two slightly older ones lying around. They will probably not have faded very much and the new ones are quite expensive (see Chapter 10).

The main thing you need for good colour calibration is confidence. I know graphic designers who, after years of saying how much they would like to do their own colour work, are still getting it all done by their repro house or printer because they don't feel confident doing it themselves.

Remember, it is unlikely that you will have to jump straight in at the deep end. Assuming right now that you do not know how to calibrate anything and that you want to end up calibrating everything, let us take it one step at a time. Start small – let your first attempt be a manageable image that is not fraught with problems to begin with. Nobody will notice if you end up doing a reasonable job. This may sound odd, since you would normally want somebody to notice if you did a reasonable job, but not in this case. If someone notices what you did, it will either be because it is just wonderful, or just awful. If you are only going to start with a small image on a page that also contains larger, more important images, it is unlikely anyone is going to appreciate the quality of calibration on the postage-stamp-sized image you worked on. If nobody notices anything, you have won – you will have been convincing. Eventually, you may want people to notice, but for now, be content with anonymity.

Also, do not imagine that your repro house/print shop is populated by beings with god-like calibration capabilities. The chances are they are using similar equipment to yours and doing similar things with it. Also, the chances are that they are much less concerned with doing a good job on your images than you are, so once you get the hang of things, you will make a better job of your work than they will.

Grey Component Replacement

Fortunately, with colour images, Adobe Photoshop is extremely helpful. The bad news is that the ways in which it is most helpful are somewhat involved (see 'Photoshop Colour Settings' on page 72) and not easy for even quite experienced users to understand. However, the great thing about the following calibration method is that it will produce good results for you without requiring you to venture into the more difficult and arcane area of Photoshop's colour settings.

First, it is necessary to set up your workstation properly. As I have pointed out before, on a PC screen, all the software packages have opaque backgrounds of bland, screen-filling neutral grey. Mac users have transparent backgrounds in nearly all their software so that the image they have loaded as their desktop is basically visible all the time. For calibration work, images need a surrounding area that is a neutral grey. On a PC, the default background in Photoshop is around a 50% grey, i.e. the RGB values are all set to 128, the halfway point between 0 and 256. However, if you open an image and pull the lower right-hand corner down to the right you will extend the frame. There are two advantages to doing this: first, you can do it on a Mac as well as on a PC, thus creating enough grey space around the image to be able to see colour more accurately; and second, the tools are active on this grey area. They can't actually do anything, as there is no image there, but they can be clicked and dragged onto the image, making it much easier to do certain kinds of work close to the image edge. The density of this grey is closer to a 25% tint, or RGB values of 192.

When you calibrate greyscale images, one of the main things you have to watch is that the shadows do not fill in. You do not need to worry about this with colour images, because the shadow density is carried by four colours instead of one. Even in very dark areas, it is unlikely that all four colours – or even three of them – will be present at a density higher than 80%. Despite that, you are still going to get good strong shadows in most images, but without any of them filling in. This is because Photoshop (usually) protects you from a problem called 'combined ink density' that most other software allows you to fall into. That is simply a figure produced by adding together the percentages at which each of the four colours is present in any particular pixel. In practice, if your combined ink density reaches around 250%, you are getting dangerously close to what is called the 'maximum ink density' – which, when reached, means that the ink will not stick to the paper any more during the printing process because there is already too much ink on it. This results in a phenomenon known in the trade as **picking**, and it makes a horrible sound like a crowd of people peeling their hands away from semi-dry gloss

GCR in Action

paint simultaneously. To avoid this problem in software programs such as Quark and InDesign, see 'Creating and Using a Rich Black' in Chapter 9.

Photoshop applies grey component replacement (GCR) as part of a **CMS (colour-management system)** when cyan, magenta and yellow are all present at fairly high densities within a single pixel. It removes them in a predetermined ratio and replaces them with black. It can do this because, at that ratio, C, M and Y combine to produce a neutral shade of grey. The higher the density of C, M and Y, the more the replacement occurs. As well as cutting down on the total ink requirements, this helps to ensure that not a single pixel hits maximum ink density.

A few years ago I was the production manager of a medium-size print shop in the US. One of our clients regularly sent us very expensive high-quality colour printing work – just the sort of thing that we normally loved to do. However, these jobs used to cause us a lot of problems, and for a long time we could not work out why.

The printers hated them. As soon as the jobs got onto the press, everything seemed to go wrong. The colours changed constantly, so the ink levels had to be continually adjusted to compensate. The result was a lot of manual quality control afterwards in the bindery. We typically had to order more paper for these jobs so that we would have enough good copies to supply the quantity ordered. Also, given the additional time we spent getting the job done, we had to add around 15% to the price.

The problems eventually turned out to have been caused by the designers who created the digital files. They were using tint books to select very rich, dense colours that used only C, M and Y. None of them contained any black at all. These colour specifications were then applied to large solid areas in the job, as backgrounds to everything else.

As already mentioned, C, M and Y are designed to be transparent, whereas black is designed to be opaque. When you are printing a transparent colour onto white paper, the white of the paper becomes part of the colour you see. When you print black, the paper does not show through, and so it is not involved with the colour you see.

If, for example, you printed a 70% tint of magenta with a perfectly even flow of ink, all the sheets you printed would look the same. If the ink flow became lighter, so would the tint, simply because the ink is transparent. If there is not so much of it there, more of the paper is able to show through. Similarly, if the ink flow increases, the tint will get darker.

Running a press is a bit like driving a car. You cannot just set the steering wheel once and hope that you will keep following the road. You have to make constant adjustments – a little to the left, a little to the right – to get where you want to go. On the press, the operator has to increase the ink a little bit, then decrease, then increase – and so on – in order to maintain a balance between the ink flow coming down onto the plate and the amount that the paper takes away in the process of getting properly printed. So minor fluctuations are happening all the time.

When you have three transparent colours combining to create a tint, all present at fairly high percentages, then even minor fluctuations will mean that your tint changes colour all the time. This means that the operator will spend all day running up and down the press trying to make adjustments to each of the colour is now carried by black – which, being opaque, is more stable even when there is some fluctuation in the ink flow. It is also much cheaper.

It is easy to try this for yourself in Photoshop. Create a foreground CMYK colour using just C, M and Y, and then remove equal percentages of magenta and yellow and a slightly higher percentage of cyan. Then add the same percentage of black as you removed of magenta and yellow. You will have to juggle things further to get them to be the same, but it can always be done. The amazing thing is that Photoshop can do this automatically in images on a pixel-by-pixel basis.

The result of all this research was that we were able to substitute our own tints for those of the designers, and the printer was able to spend the day walking rather than running. The bindery was also happy because there was no more manual sheet-by-sheet quality control right through the job. But happiest of all was the client, when told that in future the price of his work would be 15% lower.

6.1 The tint shown on the left, 90% C + 70% M + 60% Y, can be simplified – roughly – by removing all three colours at the 60% level and replacing them with a 60% black tint together with the remaining 30% C and 10% M, as shown on the right.

unit in turn to compensate. Not surprisingly, it is not much fun.

As an example, let us take a tint made up of 90% cyan, 70% magenta and 60% yellow. Not only would it be quite difficult to print, it would also get through a lot of ink. This is definitely something to consider, because the coloured inks are much more expensive than black.

However, most of the colour can actually be removed from this mix and replaced with black.

Imagine drawing a horizontal line through the tint percentages at the highest possible point at which they are all present (in this case that would be 60%) and removing everything below it, leaving behind 30% cyan, 10% magenta and no yellow at all. If the ink that has been removed (60% of C, M and Y) is replaced by a 60% tint of black, the resulting colour is close to being the same (fig. **6.1**). That's the theory. In practice, the colour would not only be slightly too light, it would also be too warm, as cyan is not as strong as yellow and magenta. If the black and cyan are increased slightly, the colour will be perfect.

What we did, of course, was to apply the theory behind GCR to remove most of the transparent coloured inks from the tint. As a result, printing will be much easier because the bulk

Highlights and Mid-tones

Alas, the highlights still need watching. As with greyscale images, you can use Image > Adjustments > Threshold to find the lightest areas, and then place a marker there with the Colour Sampler tool (see Chapter 4). If all four colours are present at less than 5%, and you are printing on an average-quality coated stock (you should adjust this figure if you are using a different paper), none of them is likely to make it onto the final printed page. In that case, you will need to adjust highlight levels to ensure that at least one of the colours will be present.

As for the mid-tones, you can use backwards calibration (see Chapter 3), which works very well, especially for greyscale images. Talk to your repro house, or whoever does your colour scanning, and get hold of a selection of digital images together with their printed results. Make sure that the images they give you were not changed in any way before being included in the page-layout program and printed. Open them in Photoshop (and tell Photoshop to use the embedded profile, if it asks) and take a long, hard look, comparing the on-screen appearance with the printed materials. You should be able to tell immediately whether or not your monitor is telling you anything close to the truth. If it is not, try adjusting it for brightness, contrast and colour. If your monitor does not have individual colour adjustments, use Adobe Gamma (to find it on either PC or Mac, see Chapter 3). However, if you have individual colour channel settings on your monitor, so much the better. Get the two images to look as close to each other as possible.

Once you know that you can more or less trust the overall picture you are seeing on screen, you will easily be able to see what adjustments are needed on any image you open. If your monitor could not completely get to where you wanted to go, at least you should have gained an idea of what kind of image appearance on screen will produce what kind of result in print.

A word of warning: it is very easy to overdo colour changes, so be careful. If your image has even a few percentage points too many or too few of any of the colours, it will stand out as being too blue, green or whatever – especially if there are other images near it on the same page that are closer to a balanced range. These imbalances are known as **colour casts**. To avoid missing these – and you would be surprised how easy that can be – I usually keep a few small images that I know are okay clearly visible on the screen while I am working with colour adjustments, just for the comparison.

If there are no colour casts in the image, and assuming you have by now taken care of the highlights, the only thing left to fix is the mid-tones. You can make an adjustment to these using the Composite channel (i.e. the one labelled 'CMYK') in

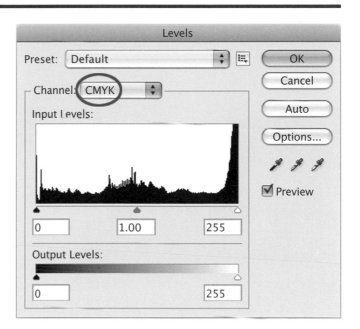

6.2 In this example, any adjustment made using the arrows underneath the histogram will affect all of the CMYK channels simultaneously.

the Levels window (fig. **6.2**). Grab the centre arrow under the histogram and pull it either to the left or right. This will involve all the colour channels together, making a balanced adjustment towards lighter or darker, but without adding any particular hue.

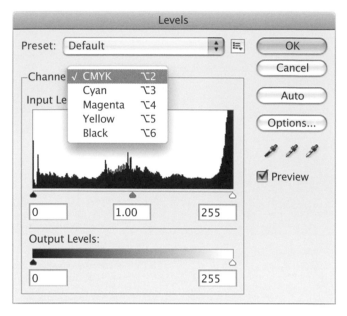

6.3 Selecting an individual colour channel for adjustment using the Levels window.

6.4 The Variations window allows for the adjustment of any component of the RGB or CMYK colour modes.

Dealing with Colour Balance

There are two kinds of colour casts. One is caused by too much of a particular colour and is fairly easy to figure out. These are 'plus-colour casts'. The other is caused by too little of a particular colour, and is much more difficult to pin down. These are 'minus-colour casts'. Our inability to make a correct decision regarding this kind of image is usually caused by all the other things in our peripheral view muddying the visual waters. Reflections on the monitor screen are also common culprits. Nor will it work to see the image on its own, with nothing else getting in the way. What you need are useful points of comparison.

If you are working with a plus-colour cast, you might be able to make a simple adjustment to just one of the colour channels. Here, colour mode is important. For instance, if the plus-colour was green, to adjust for it in CMYK mode would require changing the cyan as well as the yellow component. As you can only work on them individually in the Levels window, it would be difficult to get it right first time. However, if you change the mode to RGB you might be able to fix things with a single adjustment to the green channel.

Conversely, if a yellow adjustment is what is needed, working on the image in RGB mode would be quite difficult. You would be better off in CMYK mode.

If you want to adjust a particular channel without changing the others, go to Levels and click on the arrow to the right of the channel name at the top of the window (fig. **6.3**). You can then select the one you want to work on. Moving the arrows or making numerical adjustments will then affect only the channel you have chosen. You can also use this method to adjust individual channels in the Curves window.

A very useful area for determining colour balance is the Variations window (fig. **6.4**). If you have not used variations before, this is what to do:

Open the image you want to adjust, and then choose Image > Adjustments > Variations.

The Variations window opens to show your original image in the top left corner. Beside it is one called Current Pick. This is duplicated in the centre of the array below and also at the centre of the three images down the right-hand side.

The array gives you duplicate images with added R, G and B as well as C, M and Y, and the three on the right allow you to choose whether to lighten or darken it.

The idea is that when you click on one of the variations images, it becomes your current pick. You can click on as many choices as you want. Finally, clicking on OK accepts the changes you have made and updates your image in the main Photoshop window.

The advantage of Variations lies mostly in its ability to show you changes caused by adding preset amounts of individual colours from either the RGB or CMYK systems. But what makes it truly useful is that it shows you simultaneously how all of those adjustments would look. So it gives you the points of comparison that you need to figure out what is wrong. You can compare how the original image looks against all the others and get a really good idea of the relative appearance.

While the Variations window is a wonderful tool, the size of the thumbnail images is quite small and it is not always easy to see exactly what you are going to get. For example, I still get occasional surprises when, thinking I have made a good adjustment, I click OK and find that my image is now, for example, far too warm. Also, although darkening an image is something I often do here, I do not use this window to make images lighter. Doing so tends to be damaging; the Levels window is a much safer option.

 Every time you go into the Variations window, it is vital to remember to click on the image called Original at the top left of the screen before you start making any decisions. This clears the settings made the last time you were there, which Photoshop will have remembered and already applied to the image array.

Photoshop
Colour Settings

You might wonder why Photoshop colour settings are included here rather than *before* the chapters dealing with greyscale and colour calibration. The reason is simple. Many people will use the information presented in these chapters and find that they get along much better than they did before, but they still will not want to mess around with the colour-management zone in Photoshop or InDesign, which is a much more daunting prospect. It is an area that very few people understand, and if you do not understand it then you cannot really use it effectively. Most people would rather just leave it alone and trust that the Photoshop defaults will not get them into too much trouble. Unfortunately, you cannot rely on this being the case, and so having at least an overview of what this area can do for you is worthwhile, especially if it leads you towards making informed adjustments to your colour settings.

In the following explanation, a 'CMYK colour space' is the full range of colours that can be generated using all the possible combinations and tints of a particular set of CMYK pigments, while an 'RGB colour space' holds all the RGB colour combinations.

Certain conventions about colour have been developed by a group called the International Colour Consortium (ICC). Generally, graphics programs such as Photoshop use these conventions to determine their own colour-management workflow. These are called colour-management systems (CMS). The idea is to give consistency to your images wherever they are displayed throughout the entire work process – all the way from your screen, right up to a finished website, and even to the pages rolling off the press. Otherwise, particularly because there are many different CMYK 'spaces' out there among print shops (caused by using different inks, for example), the results are unpredictable.

Similarly, while all monitors and scanners display and capture images using RGB, not all monitors and scanners share the same RGB space – aside from which, most monitors are weak in terms of green and cyan display. So there are many variables, and making use of the Photoshop colour settings is a way of overcoming the difficulties in consistency that might otherwise arise.

A CMS setting applies a **colour profile** to an image, which tags it with a description of how the colours included within it map to a particular colour space. If you do not choose a profile, your image is untagged, and instead picks up Photoshop's current working space profile as a default CMS. This then determines how your computer will display and edit the colours. If you choose a profile, it will be applied when, for example, you change the colour mode of an image from RGB to CMYK. You can also choose whether or not to apply your resident

6.5 The Bridge icon on the Photoshop menu bar.

settings to an image that is tagged with a different profile, as it is being opened.

If you already have an image open on screen, changing the profile settings will affect only the on-screen appearance. Actually tagging an image with the resident profile can only take place during the process of being opened, and the tag is then saved when you save the image.

As the settings have stabilized over the last few versions of Photoshop, I have not included notes for versions earlier than the current CS model. Regarding these, it does not make any difference whether you have a Mac or a PC.

To enter the CMS settings area, open Adobe Bridge. This can be done by clicking on the Bridge icon on the menu bar in Illustrator, InDesign or Photoshop (fig. **6.5**). The reason for doing this in Bridge is that tags can be put into place for all three programs at the same time, in a synchronized way.

In Bridge, choose Edit > Creative Suite Colour Settings. When the Suite Colour Settings window opens, it will probably show that the current, and default, CMS is North America General Purpose 2. That is great if you live in the US and send your work out to be printed on coated paper on a web press. For the rest of us, it is not so good. Instead, scroll up the list and choose Europe Prepress 3 instead (fig. **6.6**). Click the Apply button to close the window and return to Photoshop.

NB If you reopen the window, its top area will show that your settings are now synchronized across the suite for consistent colour. If the settings are changed in any one of the applications, this area will say that the colour settings are unsynchronized.

If you are on a Mac, choose Photoshop > Colour Settings. On a PC, choose Edit > Colour Settings. In both cases, the Colour Settings window will now show that Europe Prepress 3 is in place (fig. **6.7**), and the CMYK working space will have changed to Coated FOGRA39. (Previously, it would have read US Web Coated (SWOP) v2.)

So, why would that have been a problem? The answer lies in a formidable area for the graphic designer: dot gain. In Chapter 4, this has been discussed in terms of controlling the size of the highlight and shadow dots, but here we are dealing with the main problem: how do we control what happens to the mid-point in the image tone, i.e. the 50% dot? This is important, because if we can control it, we thereby control the overall appearance of the entire image – with the exception of the highlight and shadow dots, which we have already dealt with. The amount by which the 50% value changes (and it is always an increase in density) during the printing process is the *actual* dot gain amount that is compensated for by the CMS you put into place in the Colour Settings window. And the bad

news is that on a web press, dot gain is roughly twice that of a sheet-fed press: 20% instead of 10%. If you are not sure how this will affect your work, read on.

A 50% dot going through a web press, unchanged, comes out at roughly a 70% dot. This would mean the mid-tones are dark and muddy, and the printed picture looks awful.

If a CMS profile for a web press is left in place, the 50% dot is curved down to a 30% dot (but without changing how the image looks on screen) so that during the printing process the dot gain turns it back into a 50% dot, and the picture looks great.

However, if you are printing on a sheet-fed press but using a CMS that compensates for a web press, the 50% dot is curved down to a 30% dot but only picks up 10% dot gain

6.6 The Suite Colour Settings window, with Europe Prepress 3 selected.

6.7 The Colour Settings window in Photoshop, showing the settings for Europe Prepress 3.

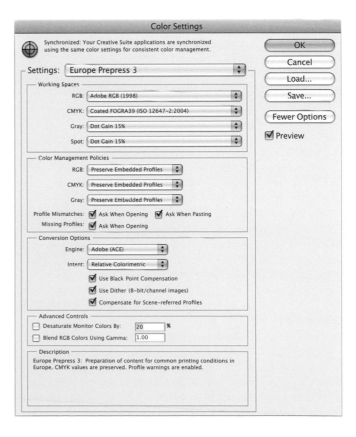

on the press… thus printing as a 40% dot, in which case the mid-tones look washed out and pale.

See the problem? Most graphic designers do not even know about this, let alone dare to change it. As a friend of mine commented, 'the CMS area is a classic example of putting the tools of genius into the hands of idiots: anyone can change a CMS, but very few people know how to do it.'

So, most of us send our work to the printer with the wrong profile in place. The printer is left with two poor choices: peel away the digital tag and try to fix it on the press, or just try to fix it on the press. Neither is the best way forward.

The key to putting the correct CMS profile in place is to talk to your printers. They should be able to tell you which CMS to choose for the best results in their shop, on their presses. If you change something without talking to them, you run the risk of having them assume that the default US web profile is part of your workflow, and adjust the ink flow accordingly. However, as this is not the case, they will probably waste a lot of paper.

If you know exactly what the dot gain is going to be, you can adjust the settings quite a lot further in Photoshop, and slightly further in Illustrator and InDesign. For instance, in all three programs, if you are printing on uncoated paper, open the Colour Settings window, click on the drop-down list for CMYK (fig. **6.8**) and choose Uncoated FOGRA29. The top section of the window will tell you that your settings are now unsynchronized, but they are unsynchronized in a good way. You can also set the dot gain values for grey and spot colours here, which is especially useful if you have been able to use the dot-gain test strip discussed in Chapter 4.

If you want to customize the settings in Photoshop even further, click on the CMYK drop-down list and choose Custom at the top. This opens the Custom CMYK window (fig. **6.9**), where 'SWOP (Coated)' will probably still appear at the top. To change it, click on the Ink Colours field and choose either Eurostandard (Coated) or Eurostandard (Uncoated), depending on the stock on which you will be printing. Here, the dot gain level can be set to a specific percentage rather than the 10% increments of the previous window. In the lower section, set the Separation Type to GCR, the Black Ink Limit to 100%, the Total Ink Limit to 300% and the UCA Amount to 0%. Leave Black Generation set to medium.

Back in the Colour Settings window, I usually leave the CMS policies to convert images to the working space in all three areas, but then check *all* the Ask boxes. This means that whenever you open an image to which another profile – or even no profile at all – has been attached, Photoshop will convert

6.8 The drop-down list showing CMYK alternatives in the Photoshop Colour Settings window.
6.9 The Custom CMYK window.

them to your chosen working profiles. By checking the three Profile boxes, you ensure that you get another chance to change your mind before any such conversion occurs, even when you are pasting areas between images with mismatched profiles.

If you cannot see the Conversion Options in the Colour Settings window, click on More Options. Choose Adobe (ACE) as the engine, and either Relative Colourmetric or Perceptual as the intent. The Adobe ACE engine is best for RGB to CMYK conversion, while the Intent compresses the RGB space into the target space while trying to retain the balance of the original. Adobe recommends using Relative Colourmetric, whereas I usually use Perceptual. Have a look at the descriptions for both, and then choose whichever one you think best. They are *both* very good!

When you are happy that everything is correct for your current job, click on Save and give your custom settings a name and a description. The description will then appear in the box at the foot of the window whenever that setting is chosen.

Calibration Test-strip Settings

You can also find your freshly saved setting, with its description, as a new CMS option in the Suite Colour Settings window ('Edit > Creative Suite Colour Settings') in Adobe Bridge. By selecting it there, it is applied to the entire Adobe suite as well as being an option available when making a high-resolution PDF from InDesign. You can thus create and save all kinds of CMS profiles, which can be applied to any work you do in the future.

Even though I believe that using the above information will help to improve the quality of image output, if you have any serious doubts then do not feel that everything will turn to garbage if you simply leave things as they are. You do not have to panic: it *is* okay to go slowly. If you are reasonably happy with your printed results, then it is not really broken and therefore might not need fixing. Do not feel that you have to change any of your settings, yet. Talk to your printer, who may be able to help you decide; if not, you could also try a technical support call to Adobe. The chances are you will still feel unsure, because this is stuff you are unlikely to have heard much about, even if you have just completed a three-year graphics degree course. If you would like to try making some basic changes but also want to tread carefully, then, if you live in the UK, simply pick one of the European defaults for your CMYK setting and do not change anything else. Similarly, if you live in the US, pick a coated or uncoated option for either sheet-fed or web and leave it at that. The sky will not fall on your head, and you will soon have added to your experience to the point that you will probably feel confident about going a little further.

In Chapter 4 I suggested creating a calibration test strip to help you figure out highlights, shadows and dot-gain levels. If you decide to make one of these in Illustrator or CorelDRAW and then open it in Photoshop to see if the tint values are accurate, you should be aware that some of the choices you will be offered as you open it could affect the tint values shown. These notes are intended to help you decide what to do.

Photoshop always checks to see whether the image you are trying to open already has an applied colour profile. If it has not, or if the assigned profile is different from the one you are currently using, you will get one or more message windows appearing prior to the file actually opening on screen. Depending on the choice you make at this point, the tint values in the image will either stay as they are or change.

Generally, for images that you wish to work on in Photoshop, this is not a problem. If you are using a particular CMS in Photoshop, and have subsequently applied backwards calibration to your monitor settings, then the combination of the two is already taking care of dot gain in a satisfactory way. But in the case of a calibration test strip, it is important that none of the tint values change at all, and so in this case the CMS must not be allowed to get in the way.

First, do not let the source program in which you create the strip attach a colour profile to it. If you are going to use Adobe Illustrator, go to Edit > Assign profile and check the 'Don't colour manage this document' button. If you are using CorelDRAW, when you export the file as a TIFF, make sure that the Use Colour Profile box is not selected (for more about the TIFF file format, see Chapter 7). Then, when you open the resulting file in Photoshop, choose the 'Leave as is' option.

If, for example, you had instead picked Dot Gain 10%, the tint values would have undergone major changes. The calibration test-strip tint values between 0–10% would have become 0–6%. The 50% tint would be 34%, and the 91–100% tints would become 76–100%. You can see from these figures just how much a CMS can change things, and why it is important to stop it from making any adjustments to your test strip.

However, if you choose the 'Leave as is' option and then resave the file as a TIFF image, when you open it up again you will see another window telling you that the 'Document has an embedded profile that does not match the current grey working space' box. Of the three choices it then offers, 'Use the embedded profile [instead of the working space]' will result in no change to the original tints; 'Convert document's colours to the working space' results in the same kind of changes already noted above; and 'Discard the embedded profile [do not colour manage]' also leaves the tints unchanged.

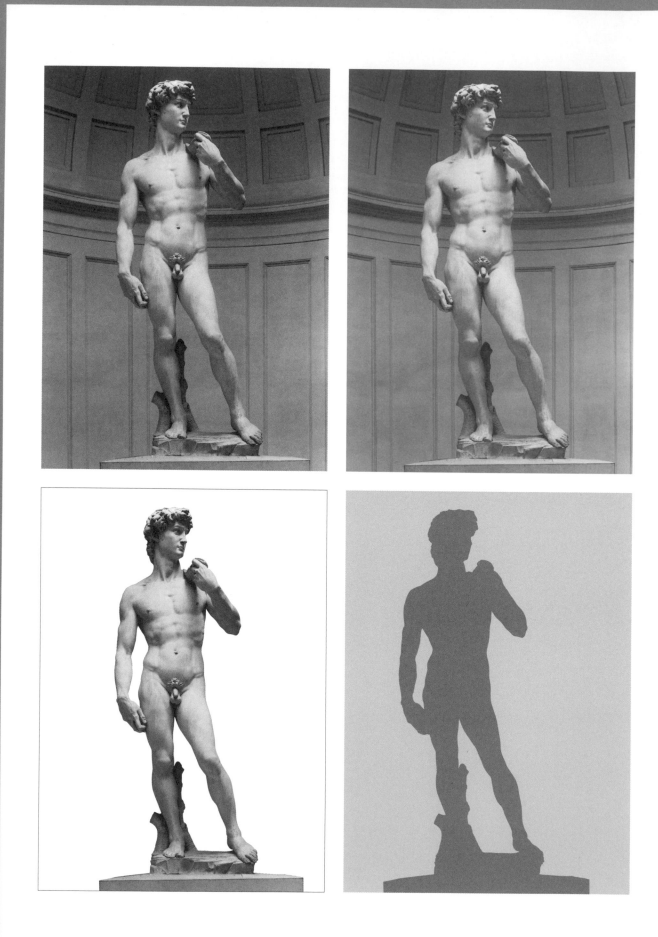

Good and Bad Image Formats… and Others!

7

As a graphic designer it is important that you understand what kind of image is appropriate to use for what purpose. For instance, you cannot use a TIFF image on a website, nor would you want to use a GIF image for print.

There are also a variety of image types that, if you are using InDesign for your page layout, are no longer required. Being able to leave them behind allows you to also leave behind some potential problems that have plagued the design industry for years. EPS files, for instance, long held to be 'the preferred image format on a Mac' (for no good reason) are no longer needed at all. Nor are DCS files or duotones. All the same results can now be achieved in a better, more stable and therefore less stressful way. And there is also a 'special case': JPEGs. These can be used for print, and also on the web. But to use JPEGs properly, you will need to know enough about them to avoid any problems.

Opposite: What's the best image format for a clipping path? How about a duotone? What if it's a CMYK run? This chapter has the answers…

Good Image Formats

Here we take a look at the different kinds of images commonly available to a graphic designer with a view to figuring out which ones are okay to use and which ones are best to ignore. We will start with the good ones.

As far as offset printing is concerned, there are only three image formats that you should consider using in a page layout: TIFF files, various kinds of EPS files, and PSD files. And that is all. Forget JPEG (almost always, anyway – JPEG images can *sometimes* be used, but they fall into a 'special case' category, hence the inclusion of '...and others!' in the chapter title). If you plan on using JPEGs, please read that section carefully as they are not generally a print-friendly format (unless you are using your desktop inkjet machine, or something similar). You should also forget GIF, PNG and BMP. That is not to say that the image cannot be one of those formats at some point, but just that they are not the formats to send to print.

You can also use PDF files, but as they can contain entire layouts rather than being single images they are also a special case – again, see below.

7.1 The TIFF Options window, showing the compression methods available.

TIFF (tagged image file format)

TIFF (shortened to 'TIF' on a PC) files can be simple bitmaps (two-colour images in which each pixel can be just one of the colours), greyscale images, RGB or CMYK. The important thing about them is that each pixel is allowed to be anything it wants to be within the given range of the image and the applied colour profile. As uncompressed images, they tend to be quite large; a full-bleed A4 CMYK TIFF at 300dpi can be anything between 30 and 40MB. In Photoshop there is a lossless (i.e. no loss of quality) compression option for TIFF files called LZW (Lemple-Zif-Welch). While it saves on disk space it can sometimes cause problems for the printer, so try to avoid using TIFF files in a page layout that have the compression option still attached. Open them and resave, turning the LZW button off during the process (fig. **7.1**). I avoid this option in general because several times now I have saved something as TIFF using LZW, only to end up with a corrupted image that cannot be opened at all.

Although it is possible to save a multi-layer image in TIFF format, I almost always save multi-layered files in Photoshop format (PSD), and only 'flattened' (i.e. single-layer) images as TIFF files. An exception to this is when I place text on top of an image in Photoshop. In that case, keeping editable text on its own layer preserves it as vector information. This means that when the result is placed into a page layout, the text will be able to print out at the maximum resolution of a PostScript printer rather than being held to the same resolution as the image. This is particularly useful when the text involved is small. However, if it is above 40pt I usually flatten the text layer into the background, as at that size the appearance will still be very good even though the text is now made up of pixels rather than vector information.

Otherwise, TIFF files are generally simple. They do not even need a PostScript printer to output them. The data just gets processed, one pixel at a time, until the whole thing is done. I cannot remember ever having a problem with a simple TIFF. Problems are always caused by something else.

EPS (encapsulated PostScript)

While EPS files can be useful, I do not agree with people who tell me that EPS is the preferred image format for everything. They have their uses, but they also have some disadvantages, especially for Quark users.

EPS files can be one of two basic kinds: vector or bitmap. Bitmapped EPS files are like TIFFs in that they are resolution-dependent, i.e. they have a fixed resolution based on the number of pixels there are to the inch. The amount of detail they can display is limited to the detail captured during their creation, whether it was by scanner, digital camera or Photoshop. Increasing the resolution later merely spreads the original data over more pixels. This might smooth the pixelated edges somewhat, but it does not add any detail beyond what was there to begin with.

However, if you have drawn an object in Adobe Illustrator and saved it as an EPS file, or drawn the same thing in CorelDRAW and exported it as an Adobe Illustrator or EPS file, then it is a vector image and not a bitmap. This means it is not resolution-dependent and can instead be infinitely scaled to any size. Even if the image was drawn on a tiny section of the page, it can be enlarged to fit on the side of a bus – and it would look as sharp and clean as if you had zoomed in to view the original. Better still, both these formats support a transparent background, so you can import them into a page layout and place them on top of an existing background with no problem.

EPS files of this kind are also quite small – and it can be a bit of a shock to discover that the logo that you have created and that will soon be screenprinted, three metres (nine feet) tall, onto the side of a supermarket lorry is only 18kb.

Other things you should know about EPS files

There are, as I mentioned, some disadvantages with EPS files.

Generally, a true EPS image can only be seen when it is printed. What you see in Quark or InDesign is actually the 'preview', or '**image header**'. This is a low(er)-resolution TIFF, created as the EPS file is being saved (fig. **7.2**). This lies on top of the PostScript code so that you can at least see where the image has been placed, and roughly how it looks. I say 'roughly', because the maximum depth for an image header is usually 8-bit, so it can only show you 256 colours – much like a GIF. This means that what you have to look at while you are working has a quality level that is less than superb, especially in Quark, where it will look grainy and/or low-resolution. InDesign does rather better, and its display is just about indistinguishable from a TIFF. The true, high-quality image beneath it only appears when it is ripped ('raster image processed' – when the vector information of the EPS file is turned into halftone dots) with a PostScript printer.

Personally, I prefer to work with high-resolution images on screen no matter what program I am working in. It just helps the creative flow. If I am constantly having to deal with lower image quality on screen while I am trying to design something, things tend not to flow as well as they otherwise might.

7.2 The EPS Options window, which determines the preview image in a layout.

Vector images

Illustrator files can generally be copied and pasted straight into InDesign as editable vector objects. Indeed, as the Pen tool in InDesign is exactly the same as it is in Illustrator, the imported object does not appear in the Links window as InDesign considers it to be a 'native' object. It can therefore be edited further on the InDesign page. More complex objects may need to be saved in '.ai' (Adobe Illustrator) format and placed in the same way as other images. In that case, additional editing in InDesign will not be possible.

There is no need to add **clipping paths** to files saved in .ai format. It is much easier simply to open them in Illustrator (or import them into CorelDRAW), remove any unwanted background, and resave them in the same format. Vector images saved in encapsulated PostScript (.EPS) format, however, might pose some problems. Even though you can import them into Illustrator or CorelDRAW, you cannot do anything with them in either program other than resize them on the page. In this case, there is no alternative but to open them in Photoshop in order to deal with unwanted background areas. Doing so immediately makes them resolution-dependent, which unfortunately negates their main advantage, i.e. infinite scaleability. In fact, when you try to open an EPS image, Photoshop will immediately ask for the size and resolution at which you want it to be opened. When you enter your requirements and click OK, the EPS information gets rasterized into pixels at the resolution you have specified. If your vector image contains fine outlines that are made up of colour tints, these will get rasterized into dots, too, which will probably make them look fuzzy.

Clipping paths

A clipping path is a vector outline drawn on an image that acts as a mask. When the image is placed into a page layout, only the parts of it enclosed by the outline can appear.

Clipping paths are usually created either in Photoshop or in the page-layout program being used for final document assembly. If a clipping path has too many **nodes** in it (i.e. points that anchor the path into a particular shape), the PostScript code involved can overload the printer to the point where it can no longer print. But for me the main disadvantage is that vector paths ignore pixels and cut right across them, creating an edge that is *not* anti-aliased and can therefore look as if it were cut out with scissors and pasted into place.

Anti-aliasing is a slight falling off of tone around the edge of an element that gives it a slightly soft edge and enables it to blend in visually with the rest of the image much more than would otherwise be possible. Photoshop typically applies it as a default when you copy and paste selections. It is also applied to items such as menu text on your computer screen, thus allowing it to have a smooth appearance despite being part of a comparatively low-resolution display.

The easiest place to create a clipping path is in Photoshop, as a selection made here can be transformed into a path. This can save a lot of time, as it is usually much faster to create a selection of the desired area than it is to draw a path around it. The path can then be saved as a clipping path.

7.3 The original image prior to the generation of the vector path.

7.4 For accurate selections on difficult backgrounds I usually use a combination of the Magic Wand and Freehand Lasso tools.

Fig. **7.3** shows a dancing figure against a fantasy background. To place the figure, without the background, on a page in InDesign you would perform the following operations.

Using a combination of the Magic Wand tool and the Freehand Lasso tool, create a selection shape around the figure (fig. **7.4**). To turn the selection into a path, you now have two choices.

First, click on the Options button at the top right of the Paths window (fig. **7.5**) in Photoshop and select Make Work Path. Doing this gives you the chance to enter a tolerance factor. The tightest tolerance available is 0.5 pixels; this will create a path that will be the closest possible to your original selection, but will probably contain hundreds of anchor points holding it into

shape. An entry of 0.8 will make it much smoother, though still reasonably close to your selection shape. Progressively larger values smooth the resulting path ever further, right up to a value of 10, when it will be very loose indeed.

Second, if you click on the 'Make work path from selection' button at the foot of the Paths window, Photoshop will remember the same tolerance factor chosen the last time a work path was created and apply that without giving you further options.

Either way, a work path is created in the Paths window (fig. **7.6**), and the selection is converted into a vector path (fig. **7.7**). This will be the basis of the clipping path.

7.5 The Options button in the Paths window. The Make Work Path window, where you can set a Tolerance (an accuracy factor) for the path it then generates, based on your selection

7.6 (Inset) The new work path, in the Paths window.
7.7 The work path replaces the selection on the image.

NB Each point at which the path suddenly changes direction involves a node that anchors it in place, so if you choose 0.5 as your tolerance factor you could be creating an object that is too complex to print. A setting of 0.8 or 1.0 smooths things out without losing the overall shape of your selection, and this is usually a better choice. However, it is a good idea to zoom in and check it, in case you decide it needs further editing.

Click on the Options button again and choose Save Path (fig. **7.8**). You will be offered the names of 'Path 1', 'Path 2' and so on, but you can call them whatever you want. Doing this changes the path name in the Paths window (fig. **7.9**). Having saved the path, click on the Options button again and choose Clipping Path, which until now has been greyed-out. You will be asked to choose which path to apply the property to (fig. **7.10**). If your image has several paths drawn on it, you can select from the list. Leave the 'Flatness: device pixels' window blank, as then the entire image will print to the highest possible resolution of the target printer.

Save the image and place it into a page layout to see the result (fig. **7.11**).

Clipping paths work in several file formats, including EPS, TIFF and PSD (see below).

7.8 (Inset) The work path should then be saved as a named path, to which 'clipping' attributes can be applied.
7.9 The work path has now been saved as 'Path 1'.

7.10 Select which path to apply the clipping property to.
7.11 The final result shown in an InDesign layout.

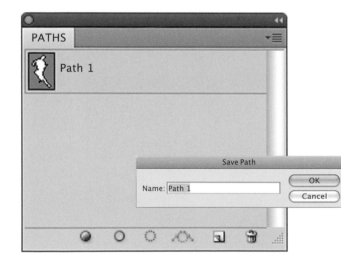

Duotones, DCS and PDF files

There are three other kinds of EPS files that deserve a special mention: **duotones**, which are two-colour images, typically made up of black plus a Pantone colour (Pantone colours are discussed in Chapter 10); DCS (desktop colour separation) files; and PDF files.

Duotones

Duotones, alas, tend to be calibrated poorly or not at all, resulting in a muddy appearance in the mid-tones. This usually happens because both the colour channels in the image have been left with the same spread of emphasis.

To convert an image into a duotone it must first be rendered as greyscale. In the example shown in fig. **7.12**, I used Images > Adjustments > Black & White to make the conversion (fig. **7.13**). Then I chose Images > Mode > Duotone.

In the Duotone Options window (fig. **7.14**), click on the drop-down arrow next to the Type field and choose Duotone. You can also create one-, three- and four-colour images using a custom palette.

As the first colour in a duotone is typically black, that colour will already be chosen – although of course you can change this by clicking on the chip. To choose the second colour, click in the white square directly below the black colour chip. This opens the Colour Libraries window (fig. **7.15**), in which you can

---

7.12 The original image, prior to duotone conversion.

7.13 The colour image is first converted to greyscale.
7.14 The Duotone Options window, where you can create images containing between one and four colours, all of which can be other than CMYK.

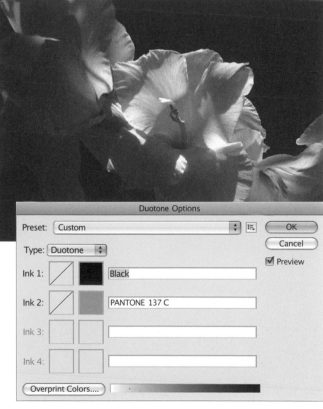

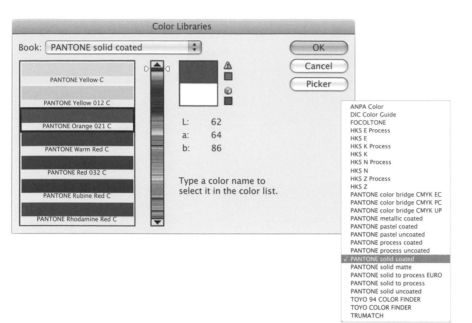

7.15 The Colour Libraries window, which includes the Pantone Solid Coated library and many more.
7.16 (Inset) The libraries list shows collections of non-CMYK colours used around the world, including the Pantone series, commonly used in the USA and Europe, and Toyo, commonly used in Asia.

7.17 In a new duotone, the second colour is usually too strong at first.
7.18 (Inset) The Duotone Curve window acts in a very similar way to the Curves window.

7.19 The end result is much more subtle.

select the type of library by clicking on the drop-down list (fig. **7.16**) in the top left corner. If, as is likely, you choose the Pantone Solid Coated library and you know which colour you want, just type the appropriate number and it will be selected. Otherwise, you can choose from the list.

It is extremely likely that the image will appear quite dark and heavy in the second colour (fig. **7.17**). However, if you 'bend' the mid-tone region of the lighter colour to make it somewhat brighter, this problem can be avoided. This is very much like making an adjustment using Curves. Click on the square with the diagonal line crossing it, directly to the left of your Pantone colour chip, to open the Duotone Curve window (fig. **7.18**). To lighten the second colour, pull the curve into the shape shown. The image will update when you release the mouse button, and the result should be a much more subtle image (fig. **7.19**). If needed, the black channel can also be adjusted using the same method.

Images in duotone format should be saved either as a Photoshop EPS or PSD file. The EPS format, in this case a two-channel image, requires that you choose a preview image type. For more details, see the EPS section, above. If it is saved in PSD format the preview is not needed.

Duotones containing spot (Pantone) colours that have been placed into a page layout are included as part of the composite when a PDF document is created. If you are in doubt as to whether the spot colours actually made it into the file, open it in Adobe Acrobat Pro. Choose Advanced > Print Production > Output Preview, where you should see any Pantone colours used listed beneath the process colours. Alternatively, place the resulting PDF file into a new Quark or InDesign document, which immediately adds the required Pantone colours to the colour swatches.

If you want to use a duotone as part of a CMYK print run, do not leave it in its two-colour EPS format or you will be adding the Pantone to the job as a fifth colour – and therefore also adding a lot of additional expense. Instead, convert the duotone image into CMYK format, and save it as a TIFF.

DCS (desktop colour separations)
Desktop colour separations are another form of the EPS file format. There are two versions: DCS1 and **DCS2**.

DCS1 images are made up of five separate files: the four individual elements of the colour separation plus a preview composite. I do not use DCS1 files at all. Instead, I convert any such files into TIFF (or occasionally EPS) format and use that instead.

DCS2 format supports spot channel colours in addition to the four-colour separation and preview, and can be saved either in a multi-file format or as a single composite image.

If you have to add a spot (Pantone) colour to a CMYK image, DCS2 used to be the only format that could do it. However, it is now also possible to use either a PSD or Photoshop PDF file instead, neither of which restricts the resulting view to a 256-colour preview in the page layout. For more on the use of Pantone colours and the DCS2 format, see 'Typical scenario 3' in Chapter 10.

PDF (portable document format)
Anything saved as a PDF file can be placed into InDesign or QuarkXPress. After all, a PDF file is an image captured in a PostScript format, and therefore very similar to EPS and DCS files. And, just like EPS and DCS files, there is usually nothing very useful that you can do to edit it once it has been created and saved. If the file from which it was generated contained mistakes, you usually get everything, warts and all, back from the printer – it is unlikely that they will check it very thoroughly. This means that a PDF file can end up containing RGB colours, seriously compressed images, no trapping, and sometimes the fonts will have been embedded and sometimes not.

A spot-colour image can be saved as a Photoshop PDF file as well as in DCS2 or PSD formats. When placed into the page layout in InDesign, for example, the spot colour itself will not usually be visible even though the relevant colour is immediately added to the Swatches window. However, when the layout is itself exported as a PDF, the spot colour can be seen as an overlaid addition by choosing Advanced > Print Production > Output Preview.

Better news is that PDF files, just like other EPS files, can contain both vector and bitmapped images. This makes them very versatile and useful, especially if you want to send your printer a high-resolution file that needs nothing else done to it prior to film or plate output. See Chapter 12 for more information about creating PDF files.

You can open a single-page PDF file, or one page of a multi-page PDF file, in Photoshop. However, if you do this, it is opened as an EPS file: also, the whole thing will be converted into a bitmap, including all the text *and* vector information. Multiple pages of a PDF document can be placed into an InDesign file where vector information will be retained, and it can even be re-exported as a second PDF.

PSD files

Typically, a PSD file is a multi-layer format used to generate the appearance of the final image, whether it is for print or web use. Layers are created, objects placed on them, and various operations performed to produce the desired composite image made up from all the visible layers. When ready, it can be saved in this multi-layered format as a PSD (for archiving and possible future use) and also flattened into a single layer prior to saving as a TIFF, JPEG or whatever.

It is also possible to place high-resolution CMYK PSD files into page layouts and turn layers on or off to produce the desired appearance. So, if one of the layers contains an image that has

an elliptical feathered edge 20 pixels wide on an otherwise transparent background, it can be used as the placed image if the other layers are switched off. This is a huge step forward for the designer, as previously this kind of appearance required the building of a larger composite image, incorporating both the feathered layer *and* the background elements over which it was placed. Only then could the whole thing be imported into the page layout. Any additional adjustment of any of the elements would require deleting it from the page layout, reopening it in Photoshop, making the changes, saving it again and reimporting it.

In the example, the background layer in the original image (fig. **7.20**) was converted into a 'normal' layer by double-clicking on it and then on OK, as doing this allows the generation of

7.20 The original file.

7.21 A rectangular selection is made.

transparent areas. Then a rectangular selection was made (fig. **7.21**). This was given a feathered edge in Photoshop, using the Refine Edge window (fig. **7.22**).

In InDesign, PSD file layers can either be selected as the image is placed, or subsequently. To enable selection of layers when placed, the Show Import Options box should be checked in the window that opens after choosing File > Place. This opens the Image Import Options window, where layers can be turned on and off to generate the correct preview. If the file has already been placed, select it and then choose Object > Object Layer Options (fig. **7.23**), which also allows you to switch layers on and off. The file can then be placed into a page layout (fig. **7.24**).

For me, PSD files now come under the category of 'best

of the whole lot' in terms of printability. Not only can you work with the various layers in the page layout, you can also save duotones, clipping paths and even spot-colour channels in this format. In the case of duotones and spot channels, as soon as the image is placed into a page layout the relevant Pantone colours appear in the Swatches window. Clipping path images show exactly as they would as an EPS file, except that you will not be looking at a 256-colour preview: a PSD file allows you to see the actual image.

NB When saving a duotone in PSD format it is still necessary to adjust the strength of the Pantone colour or it is likely to be too strong. See the calibration notes in the Duotone section, above.

7.22 The selection is given a feathered edge using the Refine Edge window.

7.23 (Inset) The Object Layer Options window in InDesign, in which you can turn layers in a PSD file on and off to generate a specific appearance.
7.24 The final result, placed into an InDesign layout.

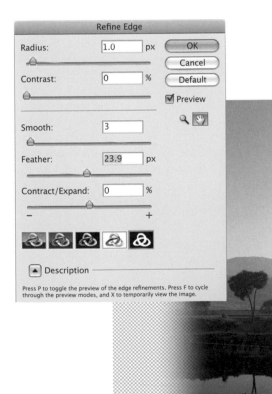

Bad Image Formats

Most of the 'bad' file formats will print quite well on a desktop system, but nevertheless should not be included in files sent out for offset printing. The main reason for this is that non-PostScript desktop printers, both laser and inkjet, are built to handle only RGB images and *not* CMYK. However, higher-level PostScript systems (such as imagesetters) are built to deal with CMYK but not with RGB. Greyscale images print well on either system.

Many slide viewers that we may use to open images on our computers display a very reasonable on-screen view of an RGB image, whereas CMYK images usually look very odd. Because of this, it is extremely important to check not only that you are using the correct kind of image but also that you make sure it is in CMYK format before sending it out. The only exception to this should be when RGB JPEGs are being added to, for example, an InDesign page layout that is then being converted to a CMYK PDF output. In that case, all the RGB data is overwritten by the CMYK profile, and as the resulting images become part of the PDF file they are no longer present as JPEGs. This method can result in unwanted colour changes as the mode of the images converts, and should be used only when there is no reasonable alternative.

PNG (portable network graphics)

PNG is a compressed image format used for images placed on websites. It can contain the same range of colours as an RGB JPEG, but can also support 256 levels of transparency. It therefore contains the widest range of potential of any of the web image formats. Unfortunately, this means that it is also the biggest image format, and it should be used only when its attributes make it the only possible choice.

GIF (graphics interchange format)

GIF is a great format for websites, especially for images that can be made up of a small number of colours and/or large areas of flat colour – maps, for example, or single-colour text headings with a drop shadow applied. Do not use the GIF format for images with lots of colour graduations such as continuous-tone images. This is the more regular 'photo' type of image, and although they can be saved in GIF format easily enough, you will end up with much bigger files than if you had saved them as a JPEG.

GIF files are in **indexed colour** format, which means they can display a maximum of 256 colours – and that is it. However, they can be *any* 256 colours. For example, when you save an image with perhaps several thousand different colours in GIF format, the 256 commonest colours in the original will become the entire palette. If more colours are needed to give a closer approximation to the original, GIF files can dither them together – which means a scattering of one of the colours is thrown in among the pixels of another, creating an illusion of a blend of the two when looked at from a distance. Dithering is a very memory-intensive way of producing additional colours and using it will usually produce a considerably larger file size.

To see the colours your GIF file contains, choose File > Save for Web & Devices in Photoshop. In the Optimize window, choose GIF as the file type, and set the Colour Table display to 256, the maximum number of colours possible; however, it *can* be as low as 2. Also, one colour can be designated as being transparent. You can select colours and delete them, one at a time, to see if the image suddenly degrades beyond what you are happy with, thus reducing the image to as few colours as you can possibly get away with. If you can get away with 8, 16, 32 or even 64 colours then your image will be substantially smaller, in terms of file size, than if you saved the same thing in JPEG format.

Sometimes it is possible to change a GIF into a reasonably good TIFF that can be used in a four-colour print run. It either has to be a large enough image to make a successful conversion into a TIFF, or you need to use it considerably smaller than its original size. The results have a tendency to look grainy because of the limitations on the number of colours imposed by the GIF format. If in doubt, convert a copy to an RGB TIFF and try printing it on a high-resolution inkjet machine (i.e. an inkjet that can print at a resolution of at least 720dpi) to get some idea of how it might look in print.

...and the 'Other' Category

JPEG (joint photographic experts group)

JPEGs (shortened to 'JPG' on a PC, as a maximum of three letters is allowed for the file extension), like TIFFs, can utilize a range of up to 16.7 million colours in RGB format and 4.5 billion in CMYK. However, unlike TIFFs, JPFG is a lossy format, which means that, at whatever quality level you choose to save it, you are losing information that you will never get back. Each time the image is resaved, you lose a little more. At a high-quality level, this is not a huge problem. At a low level, it is horrible.

If you save a file as a JPEG you have the option of selecting, in Photoshop, any one of thirteen quality levels (0 to 12, 0 being the lowest). To see for yourself what a lossy form of compression can do to an image, try the following.

Crop a small section from an image. Try to select something with a range of 'busy' detail and smooth detail – the skyline area of a building is ideal, as shown in fig. **7.25**. Make a duplicate, and then save one at a high-quality level (10 or more) and the other at the '0' quality level.

Once you have saved the image at '0' quality you will have to close the low-quality version and reopen it in order to see the changes. Even then, you may not see a great deal of difference between the two images until you zoom in. But then the differences are obvious.

Saving as a JPEG – at any quality level – divides the image into squares, each measuring 8 pixels on a side. An **algorithm** (a pattern, basically) is applied to each of these squares. The higher the quality level, the more complex the algorithm. If it has been saved at level 10 or higher and then resaved as a TIFF file for printing, very few people would be able to tell from the final printed image – especially without the original to compare it to – that it was ever saved as a JPEG. At level 12, it's almost impossible to distinguish it from a TIFF (fig. **7.26**). At level 0, it is another matter altogether. The 'pattern' at this level is so simple that there is only vague detail left in any of the squares. Also, because of this simplicity, you can end up with a pinkish square next to a greenish square, next to a bluish square – it is as if each becomes a completely separate mini-image that takes little or no notice of its surroundings. Where a square overlaps both a detailed area and a flat area, the flat area gets disturbed because the turbulence of the detail affects the whole pattern. The result is called **artifacting**, and it makes it look as if every object in the image is generating a heat haze.

There is never going to be a good reason for saving an image as a medium- to low-quality level JPEG. If you need a smaller file size, use **optimization** instead (see next page).

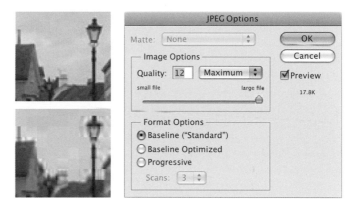

7.25 (Left) Above, the image has been saved as a level 10 quality JPEG on a scale of 0–12. Below, it has been saved at level 0. Both are enlarged so the pixels are visible.
7.26 Saving a JPEG image at quality level 12 makes it as good, visually, as a TIFF.

Otherwise, save at the highest quality level possible.

Incidentally, when saving a JPEG, only choose one of the 'progressive' settings if you are saving it for website display. This allows an image to load on screen at very low resolution quite quickly, then gradually update itself to the complete image in either two, three or four more passes. Therefore its only purpose is to give viewers something to look at in an attempt to prevent them from getting bored and deciding to go to a different website instead. The progressive setting has no place in the world of print.

The reason I have included JPEGs in 'other' is that it is *sometimes* OK to add them to an InDesign file that is being output as a PDF. In this case, they can *even be present in RGB format* – as long as the colour-management system in place, when creating the PDF, converts all the objects in the document to a CMYK profile (see the Adobe Acrobat section in Chapter 12). While this *can* be done, it *should not* be done unless there is really no alternative: whenever an RGB image is converted to CMYK, unwanted colour shifts are a likely result.

I am not going to detail the uses of other image formats because this book is primarily concerned with commercial printing issues. Web image formats have been included because they are so common, and also because they will usually cause problems when included in a commercial printing workflow. If in doubt, zoom in and take a close look at the quality of detail before you decide to use one, but make sure you convert it to either TIFF or PSD or one of the EPS formats before doing so – and check whether it is RGB or CMYK.

Images from the Web: Optimization and Resolution

It is really not a good idea just to download whatever you like from the web and use it. If you do, you may find yourself on the receiving end of a lawsuit. Before going ahead, make sure you have permission from the owner of the copyright. Otherwise it could be a very costly mistake.

Assuming you have received the go-ahead, you should also use the opportunity to request a better copy of the image you want to use. Otherwise, what you are left with will only very rarely be suitable for printing. This is for several reasons: web images are always RGB or 'indexed colour' (the GIF format); they have always been saved as JPEGs, GIFs or PNGs; and their resolution is usually described as being 72dpi – much too low to be of use unless you shrink the image to a smaller physical size in order to increase resolution. Besides that, if it is a JPEG it has probably been saved at a lower-quality setting, rather than through optimization, in order to make the file size smaller.

It is a common misconception that '72dpi' is so-named because it is the resolution of our screens. In fact, PC screens have had a resolution of 96dpi for ages, and Macs, which used to be 72dpi, have now caught up. However, the wheels of the graphics industry are slow to turn and we are likely to be referring to web resolution as 72dpi for years to come. This means that if you want an image to display at 10cm (4in) wide on a website, you will need to make sure it is 378 pixels wide and not 283, which was the number required for a 10cm (4in) image at 72dpi. If you do not do this, the image will appear smaller than you intended on *all* PCs, and most Macs.

Optimization

Optimization is not yet a universal practice, so you might be lucky enough to find that the image you want to use is actually fairly high quality. If not, an optimized image is a better starting point than if someone has tried to decrease the file size merely by saving the JPEG at a lower quality level. When that happens, the image is seriously damaged. Optimization, on the other hand, decreases the file size by a much greater amount, but – oddly enough – leaves the image appearance much closer to the original.

Think of it like this: your image has a surface, which you can see, and a depth, which you cannot see. If you save at lower and lower quality levels, you are removing detail from the surface and leaving distortion ('artifacting') in its place. If you optimize it instead, you are whittling away at the unseen depths and leaving the surface more or less undisturbed.

As an example, let us take the image that I used previously

7.27 The one on the right is the optimized image.

to demonstrate the effects of JPEG compression. Clearly, the image saved at quality level 10 was far superior to the one saved at level 0 – and yet in terms of file size, the level 10 image was 13kb, while the level 0 image was only 11kb. Not a huge difference – certainly not a very useful difference. The optimized image, on the other hand, was 3kb, and not visibly different. I have resaved it as a TIFF file in order to be able to print it, and here it is next to the original (fig. **7.27**). Both have been enlarged so that seeing any differences between them *should* be easier. Can you tell which is which?

Obviously, if you have to use a web image, you are going to be much better off if you can use an image that has been carefully optimized rather than one that has been damaged through being saved at a low quality level.

How to optimize an image

There is no need to optimize an image if you intend to subsequently place it into a page layout for print. However, when you need to save an image for a website, or to email a good-quality on-screen proof to someone, it is extremely useful.

After you have saved the high-resolution image as a TIFF or EPS file in Photoshop, but while the image is still open on screen, choose File > Save for Web & Devices. On the window that opens, click on the 2-up tab at the top. This displays the original image on the left, and to its right a copy. At the foot of the image is information telling you the current format and file size. You should only trust the size shown beneath the right-hand image, as the other is more likely to reflect what the image *would* be if it were saved as a TIFF – not very useful! The copy also displays the download time at various modem speeds.

In the Settings section on the right, you can choose JPEG, GIF, PNG-8 or PNG-24 as the file format.

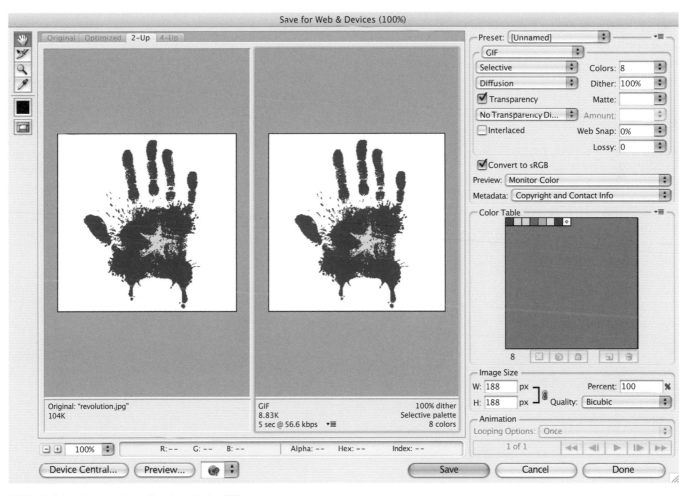

7.28 The Optimize window showing settings for an 8-colour GIF.

If you are optimizing a logo, or an image with few colours (such as a headline with a drop shadow), try GIF (fig **7.28**). This is a particularly useful format for anything that will look good with 256 colours or fewer. Additionally, one of the colours can be designated as being transparent, allowing you to delete a background.

If your image is continuous tone, i.e. like a photograph (which needs many more than 256 colours to display well), choose JPEG. The default quality setting is 60, which typically means that you will either not see any difference at all between the optimized preview and the original, or *almost* no difference. If you need the file size to be smaller, you can try reducing this

setting – but keep an eye on the quality of the image while doing so. As you make adjustments to the quality settings, the file size and download time are recalculated and the information below the copy image updates. At the same time, the result of the new settings is applied to the copy, which you can therefore compare to the unchanged original next to it. When you are happy with both the file size and the appearance of the copy, choose Save. You will then be prompted for a name and a location for the new file.

JPEGs cannot contain transparent areas and insist on being opaque rectangles. A PNG-24 file, however, can contain the entire spectrum of 16.7 million colours available to an RGB

JPEG *as well as* multiple levels of transparency. (A PNG-8 can display only one transparency level, and 256 colours – so it might as well be a GIF file.) So, a PNG-24 image can have a feathered edge that then floats on a previously coloured background in Dreamweaver, for example. The downside is that because it contains the most options, it results in a bigger file size.

Resolution

Before discussing the specifics relating to the resolution problems with web images, it would probably be useful to detail briefly the different kinds of resolution terminology that designers encounter.

Let us start with your computer screen. It has a fixed resolution of 72dpi if it's an older Mac, and 96dpi if it's a newer Mac or a PC. That 'dpi' refers to the viewing resolution only, and is the reason why images placed on websites are usually described in terms of being a particular size at a resolution of 72dpi, i.e. the lowest common denominator between the two possibilities.

If you have assembled a page layout comprising 300dpi images – i.e. 300 pixels-per-inch images – and vector text, your screen can show you nothing better than a 96dpi (or possibly 72dpi on an older Mac screen) image, though of course you can view the page at different levels of magnification by using the Zoom controls.

If you print the same page on a laser printer, it is most likely generating a 600dpi print. That means that the blobs of toner it lays down are approximately $\frac{1}{600}$ in across. This figure has nothing to do with the resolution of the elements you have placed on your page. It merely limits the detail possible in the print.

Similarly, inkjet machines typically print at resolutions of 1440dpi or greater. Again, this refers to the size of the tiny droplets of ink that they spray out in order to create the print, and has nothing whatsoever to do with the digital resolution of the images and text being printed.

Finally, the imagesetter that produces either the final film or plates from which the job will be offset printed might have a resolution of 2400dpi or greater. This allows it to generate variable dot sizes within the halftones it makes from the 300dpi images in the page layout. The resolution of these halftones is described as either **lpi** (lines per inch) or as a 'line screen', which refers to how many rows of halftone dots there are to the linear inch.

If you found that confusing, well, you have lots of company. Resolution is a confusing area for most graphic designers, and it takes a while for the information to sink in.

Web images are normally saved at 72dpi – even though most monitors are now 96dpi – but for commercial printing you need them to be 300dpi *at the size they are required to print* (for more about this, and optimum scanning values, see Chapter 8).

If you have a downloaded image that is 72dpi and 100mm (4in) wide, and you want to print at 50mm (2in) wide, it is easy to think that you have already got roughly half the resolution you need – because 72dpi over a width of 100mm (4in) requires the same number of pixels (288 of them) as 144dpi over a width of 50mm (2in), and 144 is roughly half of 300. (Digital images are generally believed by graphic designers to need a resolution of at least 300dpi in order to print using offset litho. This is not quite accurate, but is good enough for now. See Chapter 8 for more detailed information.) Actually, that is the view of the optimist. As an example, let us take an image that measures exactly one inch by one inch. If its resolution is 72dpi, how close are we to what we really need if we want to print it at that size using offset litho?

Before looking at the numbers involved in this question, I would like to mention an extremely important use of the Image Size window in Photoshop (fig. **7.29**). The default settings for this show the width and height in terms of pixels in the upper area, below which are width and height measured in the units currently selected in Preferences. Below that is the resolution field. Right now the width and height fields in both areas are linked because the Constrain Proportions box is checked. However, the resolution is not linked to width and height.

If you want to find out what the true physical size of an image of, say, 72dpi really is, uncheck the Resample Image box in the lower left corner of the window. When you do so, the top section of the window becomes locked, which means that the number of pixels in the image cannot be changed, and the resolution field becomes linked with the width and height fields in the middle section. Therefore, if any one of them is changed, the other two will change accordingly. If you highlight the '72' showing in the resolution window and type '300' in its place, the width and height will change to show you what physical size of image you have at that resolution (fig. **7.30**).

72dpi means 72 pixels for each vertical and horizontal inch of image dimension. That is a total of 72 x 72, or 5,184 pixels per square inch. At 300dpi, it is 300 x 300. That is 90,000, which is 17.361 times as many pixels. That means your original contains slightly less than $\frac{1}{17}$ of the detail you would have if you had been able to start out with an optimum-resolution scan instead. Small wonder that very few web images are worth more than a cursory glance if you are offset printing.

However, what if your image could be fairly convincingly enlarged to, say, 150dpi? In other words, a method that does a better job than merely spreading the original information over a larger number of pixels?

I have successfully taken images that, at first, seemed completely impossible to work with and ended up with images that not only printed without pixelation or colour casts, but were very convincing. It does not work all the time, but even having it work once can make it worthwhile. Find out more over the page.

7.29 The Image Size window in its default state, i.e. resolution is not linked to width and height, which are linked.

7.30 The Image Size window when the Resample Image box is unchecked: width, height and resolution are all linked to each other.

Genuine Fractals

There are several programs available that can do a better job of enlarging images than Photoshop, and if you often need to do that kind of work you should definitely consider getting hold of one. For the following example I used Genuine Fractals (by onOne software), which acts as a Photoshop plug-in and is available for both PC and Mac platforms. Genuine Fractals allows you to save an image either in a lossless or almost lossless condition.

As your web image will not bear any more loss than it has already been subjected to, let us assume you would want to save it in lossless format. When you reopen it, you can specify a resolution and size that are considerably larger than the original, and end up with a much better result than if you merely went to Image > Image Size in Photoshop and increased the pixel count. Genuine Fractals manages to keep the detail much sharper as it increases the image, which gives the appearance of detail where none existed before. For instance, if there is an object with a curved edge somewhere in the image, merely increasing the pixel count means you end up with a bigger, softer-looking curve. Genuine Fractals increases the pixel count while allowing the curve to stay sharp. That means you end up with a picture that is clearer and sharper as well as bigger – maybe even big enough to print.

Fig. **7.31** shows: left, the original 72dpi web capture; centre, a copy that has been held to the same dimensions but in which the resolution has been increased to 300dpi using Image > Image Size in Photoshop (this method is called 'interpolation', and it means that the original information has simply been spread over a larger number of pixels); and right, another copy that has also been held to the same dimensions, but saved using Genuine Fractals and then reopened at 300dpi.

Let us take a look at a slice of each of them, in the same order as shown in 7.31, but stretched to a much larger size (fig. **7.32**). See how the edges are more clearly defined on the right-hand image. Also, note how much cleaner and smoother this image looks compared to the lumpiness of the interpolated image in the centre.

Of course, lack of resolution is not the only thing getting in the way when you want to use a JPEG downloaded from the web. In almost every case, there will be severe artifacting due to the lower quality level at which it has been saved. Just about the only way to get rid of some of it is to use the Clone Stamp tool in Photoshop. The main problem areas will be those such as skies, where detail from the horizon will have influenced the 8 x 8 pixel blocks that overlap the much lighter and smoother areas of sky above them. This interference will have

been improved somewhat during the interpolation process, but now it will have to be dealt with.

You might think that it is better to deal with these areas before making them even bigger. However, even though these areas are larger after being resized using the method above, it is usually preferable to make repairs with the cloning tool *after* enlargement rather than while it is a 72dpi image. Higher resolution gives you more room to move around, and a smoother subject from which to clone better-quality tone.

The key to successful cloning is to continually redefine your source point. I cannot stress this enough. If you do not, you will see repetition patterns here and there, or areas that simply do not look right because the detail in them does not match the surrounding area.

Using GIF images

This can be very difficult because, as mentioned in Chapter 5, the GIF format allows only 256 different colours to appear in the image. Therefore, in order to create the illusion of an image with a much more extensive palette, a GIF has to scatter pixels of one of the existing colours in among the pixels of another. Then there is a good chance that our eyes will think they are seeing all the shades between the two that do not really exist.

Sometimes a GIF will have been optimized to hold fewer than 256 colours, and this of course tends to make things worse. All that can be done is to convert the image back into either RGB or CMYK mode, and then increase the image size by up to 10%. This allows the creation of new pixels that can 'choose' their colour from the entire range available in the colour space you have selected.

Unfortunately, due to the small physical dimensions of most web-based GIF images, it is unlikely that you will end up with something you are happy with in print. The only bright spot on this particular horizon is that more complex images (e.g. photographs rather than created graphics) are much more likely to have been saved as a JPEG than as a GIF, and that gives you a better chance of ending up with something that you might be able to use.

7.31 (Top Row) The original image (left) and copies enlarged using Photoshop (centre) and Genuine Fractals (right).

7.32 (Bottom Row) The same three images, enlarged to show detail.

Resolution and Scanning

Many designers already know what resolution should be used for print, but do not know why. Similarly, many know what resolution should be used for an image saved for placement on a website, but have no idea that the terminology still used is redundant because the technology has moved on – and that images will change size as a result. And then there are other kinds of resolution: we know about 'dots per inch', but what about 'lines per inch'? Are these two connected, and if so, how?

Another resolution number suddenly appears when we consider either our desktop printer, or the imagesetter producing the plates for commercial printing: suddenly we have a whole combination of numbers, each relating to some kind of resolution: 72, 150, 300, 1440, 3600. All these have a vital part to play.

Resolution can be a very confusing area unless you have an overview of what is going on. Then you can see how all these numbers relate, even though they apply to separate components of the design and printing process, and you will be able to decide exactly what is needed for a particular kind of image, heading for a particular kind of printing, even on a particular kind of paper. And, best of all, resolution issues will never confuse you again.

Opposite: Making sure you have the right resolution for the kind of output your image is heading towards is fundamentally important.

What is so Special about 300?

Most designers I have talked to about resolution have been told that they are supposed to scan everything at 300dpi, but they do not really know why. In fact, there is a formula that can be applied to any project which shows that 300dpi is not, in fact, the magic number for everything, all the time.

There are two factors involved in determining how much of the original detail an image can hold. One is the dpi, which determines how many pixels there are per inch of image. The other is the physical size of the image as it will appear on the page. If you have only one of these pieces of information then, excuse the pun, you do not have the whole picture.

For example, I am often asked to send images here and there, and told that they are needed at something like 'roughly 10 x 12 inches'. As I explained in Chapter 7, the file size of a 10 x 12in image at 72dpi is very different from a 10 x 12in image at 300dpi. Unless I am told the resolution as well as the size, I have no way of knowing exactly what is required. Sometimes Photoshop is not available to the person receiving the images, so if I send something that is seventeen times bigger than needed – and perhaps in the wrong colour mode, too – they have no way of dealing with it themselves. Also, as I do not like to send images out without the appropriate calibration, it is a great help to be told what kind of process will be used for final output.

If the final output method will be offset litho, we have to look a little closer to figure out what the dpi value really needs to be. What kind of paper is being used? If it is an uncoated paper, then the line-screen value of the halftones probably does not need to be higher than 133lpi (**Note:** that is 'lpi' – lines per inch – not 'dpi'), otherwise detail will be lost as the dots spread into each other. If, however, you are printing on a coated paper you can usually go straight up to 150lpi. Some magazine covers go as high as 175 or even 200lpi, but this is less common. The smaller the dots are, the more fiddly they are to print, and the more often the printer has to stop the presses to clean things up. So, values higher than 150lpi are used only if they are considered necessary for the quality of the result. In terms of visual effectiveness, most of us pretty much cannot see the dots at 150lpi, anyway.

The rule of thumb is to double the line-screen value that you are going to end up with and use that as the dpi at which you need the image. This is where the magic number of 300dpi comes from – it is twice the line-screen value of a halftone intended for printing on coated paper. If you have the image at that resolution, then – so long as the physical size is large enough – you are covered whether you end up printing on coated or uncoated paper, because the actual line-screen of an image is applied by the imagesetter printing the film. So it does not really matter if you have the image at a slightly higher resolution than you eventually need. All it means is that you merely have a little more detail available within the digital image than you can actually reproduce. It will not be a problem. The problem is when you have an image at a resolution that is too low, and therefore pick up less detail than you could potentially print.

Once you have decided on the correct resolution, you need to deal with the size. Of course, it is quite likely that you will not know at the outset what size you want a particular image to be. This happens to me all the time. And, if I put very many high-resolution CMYK images into a page layout, things start to slow down. If the project is a book, it may eventually mean that I have to sit and wait for the screen to redraw every time I do anything at all, which is a serious state of affairs when a deadline looms. Fortunately, there is a solution.

Creating an Efficient Workflow

The first thing to do is to process and save all the images that will be needed for the job at high resolution (300dpi is great) and in CMYK mode. This should mean that they are all as large, or larger, than you will actually require. Once you begin the layout process you will not easily be able to make any further adjustments to them, so make sure all that work has already been done. Save them all into a single folder: I usually name it 'hi-res CMYK'. Create an empty folder adjacent to it called 'lo-res RGB'.

In Photoshop, open one of the images and then choose Window > Actions (fig. **8.1**). Click on the Options button (at the top right of the window) and choose New Action. In the New Action window that opens, name it '300 CMYK to 72 RGB'

and click Record (fig. **8.2**). Now, everything you do to the open image will be recorded, so be careful!

Choose Image > Image Size and, in the window, make sure that the resolution is *not* linked to the width and height (see the Image Size window images in the previous chapter). If it is, check Resample Image in the lower left corner. Resolution should then be unlinked from the other two. I highlight the number in that field, 300, and change it to 72. Click OK, and your image will appear to change size. That is not a problem. As far as a page layout is concerned, it still has the same dimensions as before. Then, choose Image > Mode and choose RGB (fig. **8.3**). The image is now low-res RGB, but is actually exactly the same physical size as the original in terms of centimetres wide and

8.1 The Actions window.

8.2 **(Below)** The New Action window.
8.3 **(Bottom)** The Image > Mode list.

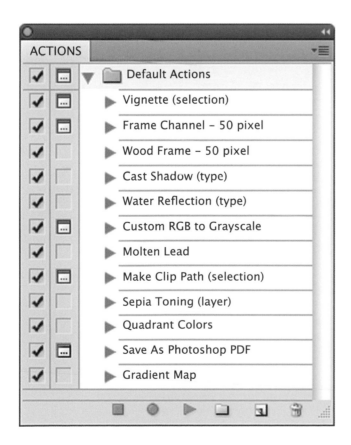

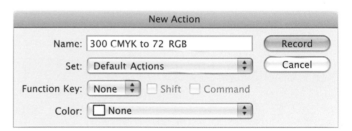

tall, and so it will occupy exactly the same area in InDesign as the original CMYK image.

Finally, close the open image *but do not save it*, or you will have just overwritten one of your high-resolution CMYK originals.

Now, still in Photoshop, choose File > Automate > Batch (fig. **8.4**). This enables you to automatically run the selected action on *all* the images in a defined 'source' location, and save the results in a 'destination' location – while you do something else.

The action you just created should appear at the top of the window; if not, choose it from the list.

The Source should be set to Folder. Then click on Choose and locate the high-res CMYK folder and select it. The 'destination' should also be a folder. Again, click Choose, find

the low-res RGB folder, and select it. Then, click OK. Photoshop will open each of the high-res CMYK images in turn, run the action on it, and save the low-res RGB result in the destination folder.

The low-res RGB images should now be used to build your design in InDesign. When it is completely finished, save the file and close it. Then, move the low-res RGB images folder, and reopen the InDesign file – which will warn you that the links to the source files are now broken, and suggest that you use the Links window to fix things. Click OK, and the file will open – apparently with all the images still in place. However, do not be misled: these are merely screen representations and are definitely not good enough to print.

8.4 (Below) The Batch window in Photoshop.
8.5 (Right) The Links window in InDesign showing the 'missing' links.

Scanning
Original Material

Open the Links window, and you will see a red 'missing link' icon opposite all the images in the list. To activate the window, click once on the top entry in the list (fig. **8.5**), then click on the 'relink' icon. This opens a file tree allowing you to identify the current location of – *not* the low-res RGB image, but the high-res CMYK image *of the same name*. Select the high-res image in the Source folder, click Open, and InDesign will find and update the links to all the other images in the layout.

Then save the file, and make the PDF. This method means that you never have to wait for the screen to redraw.

If you are scanning slides or prints in order to create the high-res CMYK files, then, to determine the correct settings for the scanner, first figure out the percentage of enlargement or reduction you need (I use a formula based on 'divide what you want by what you have' on a calculator), then double the desired halftone line-screen value to get the dpi setting. Then use that percentage and that dpi value as the scan settings for your image.

Incidentally, while scanners of amazing quality are now available at even more amazing prices, it is worth checking up on the accompanying software before buying, especially the kind of interface that is available if you want to scan directly into Photoshop. Some scanning software aims at the casual user rather than the professional, and will give you only a few presets, rather than the range of settings you need. If you cannot enter specific dpi and percentage scanning values, you would be better off with a different scanner, however tempting the deal appears to be.

8.6 (Top Row) Left: not descreened at all. Centre: descreened at 90lpi. Right: descreened at 150lpi.

8.7 (Middle Row) The RGB channels. The moiré pattern appears in the blue channel. **(Bottom Row)** The CMYK channels. The moiré pattern appears in the yellow channel.

Scanning Previously Printed Images

If you are sent an image that has been printed using the four-colour process and that you are now supposed to scan, you have two problems. The first is copyright. Does the client have the right to use this image? Check up. Otherwise, you may be liable.

The second problem is that all the correct screen angles for the CMYK colours have already been taken (see Chapter 2). If you simply scan the print again, the result will be a moiré pattern. This is because as your scanner moves across the image, it captures whole rows of pixels at a time, each one of which is called a 'sample'. The number of samples per inch (SPI) is therefore the same as the number of dots, or pixels, per inch that you have specified. All these samples put together create a grid of pixels at a new screen angle – hence the moiré.

In order to deal with this problem successfully, you have to start with the actual scanning process. Good scanners have a descreening mode. If so, there is a good chance of ending up with a decent-quality image with no moiré. Descreening modes are often presented in terms such as 'art magazine, newsletter, newsprint, custom' and so forth. These presets refer to the density of the line screen in the original image. Selecting one of these determines how much work your scanner will need to do in order to overcome the possibility of a moiré. The line screen values they usually represent are 150lpi for art magazine, 133 for newsletter, and 120 or below for newsprint.

If you know the exact line screen used to print your original, and if it is *not* 150, 133 or 120lpi, use the 'custom' option (if available) and type in the value. If 'custom' is not available, you will have to select whatever seems closest to your image.

For uncoated paper the worldwide standard for line-screen value is usually 133, but sometimes 150lpi; for coated stock it is usually 150 but sometimes 175 or even 200lpi. To see an image with and without descreening, see fig. **8.6**.

Sometimes, even if you have picked the correct lpi setting, the result will still have a visible moiré. If this happens, try rescanning at a lower lpi setting, which, as well as being faster, might also produce a better result. You will probably lose a little of the fine detail, however.

After scanning, take a look at the individual channels both before and after converting it to CMYK.

While the moiré pattern is much reduced or even completely invisible on the descreened image, something strange is happening within the individual channels while it is still in RGB mode (see fig. **8.7**). (Incidentally, to see the information in a single channel, simply click on its name in the Channels window.) The red looks better, and so does the green, but there is still a strong moiré in the blue channel. Now look at the second set of individual channels, which is how things look when the image is converted into CMYK. As you can see, while the C, M and K channels are much improved, there is a strong moiré in the yellow – however, as previously discussed, the special quality of this colour means we see the yellow but we do not see the grid, and therefore the moiré it produces remains invisible.

So the moiré in the blue channel in the RGB version becomes the moiré in the yellow channel of the CMYK version – which means that the blue moiré is just as invisible in the RGB image as the yellow moiré is in CMYK. Yet blue is visible and the moiré appears to be quite dark and strong – so why can it not be seen? The answer lies in the way the channels display information in RGB and CMYK.

RGB is made of light, whereas CMYK tends to be made of pigment. So, a dark area in a channel in a CMYK image indicates a lot of that colour. However, when something looks dark in a channel in an RGB image, it means the colour is weak there.

As the blue channel in an RGB image becomes the yellow channel in a CMYK image, and as we cannot see the yellow moiré in the CMYK version, we are also unable to see the blue moiré in RGB.

9

Trapping

If you are out walking in the woods, a trap is something you accidentally put your foot into, resulting in considerable pain and a substantial delay to your journey. In printing, 'trapping' refers to something very different – but if it is ignored or forgotten, it can also cause substantial delays while the job is reprinted, and the pain of increased costs as a result.

Trapping actually means allowing one colour to *very slightly* overprint another where the edges of the two touch. As registration between the plates on a printing press is never quite perfect, a lack of trapping will probably result in a slight gap between the colours at some point. As the gap was not part of the original design, and as it will probably stand out like a sore thumb, it is a problem. Fortunately, it a problem that is easily fixed, as long as you know what to do.

Automatic trapping specifications have been built into most good graphics software, and in some cases you can manually specify a trap if you think the automatic feature will not be enough. While these are both very helpful, most helpful of all is to know how each method functions.

Opposite: Next time you look through a magazine, and especially in the 'ads' section, see if you can see any trapping problems. They're extremely common but, with this chapter behind you, it's a trap you won't fall into.

What is Trapping?

Adobe Illustrator and CorelDRAW

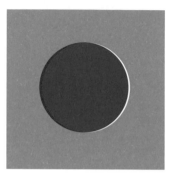

9.1 The result of misregistration between colour elements when no trap has been applied.

Most designers do not really want to think about trapping. In fact, there is really nothing to it and it is important to bear in mind that, aside from general settings, no one else is likely to take care of it for you. While you can rely on your repro house or printer to deal with trapping to an extent, you cannot expect them to scrutinize every element in your page layout and figure out whether you applied trapping to your Adobe Illustrator or CorelDRAW drawings before importing them – and, unfortunately, it is in imported images of this kind that trapping is often forgotten.

When you have adjacent areas of different colours that are going to be printed by different ink units on a press – for example, a cyan area that touches a magenta area – then unless the registration on the press is perfect, the results will not be perfect. In fact they can be seriously unpleasant. Trapping is the means by which a small overlap is applied between the colours to ensure that the very slight amount of misregistration that you are almost sure to encounter when printing is covered up. The way it is best applied depends on the software you are using.

One of the important things to know about trapping is that if you do not apply it where it is needed in Illustrator, Corel or Photoshop images, the page-layout software cannot apply it to them afterwards. Nor, except for a few very rare exceptions, can the imagesetter running the subsequent plates or film. As technology advances, trapping will become less of an issue. Some **RIP** (raster image processing – the means by which vector information, i.e a PostScript or PDF file, is converted into a printable 'raster' image, i.e. one made up of the dots output by the imaging device) systems can apply trapping to PDF documents intelligently, even when the individual elements in the page layout had no trapping applied to them prior to being imported. This is still uncommon, but if your printer can deal with it, make sure you turn off all the trapping settings in all the software you use for your page assembly, otherwise their output method may apply it a second time. For most of us, however, this is not an option. Trapping still needs to be taken care of, and we especially need to apply it to each source file using the software in which it was created. Only then will it be able to carry through to the final page layout.

In Photoshop, you cannot add a trap value unless you are working with a CMYK image – which makes sense, as it is only on a printing press that trapping is important. However, as you add your own traps in Illustrator or Corel, you are not constrained by the same laws and can apply them to RGB-coloured elements. This is a pity, and these drawing programs could avoid some of the pitfalls for designers by restricting them to CMYK colours as part of each 'new document' set-up.

I have chosen these rather lurid colours as an example of misregistration (fig. **9.1**) because they just happen to be two components of the CMYK system and are printed by different ink units on the press. If I were actually picking colours for a two-colour print job, I would probably select something more tasteful from the Pantone book.

Modern printing presses are fantastic pieces of engineering and, in the hands of a good operator, it is possible to put a cyan dot right on top of a magenta dot that is right on top of a yellow dot, and so on. But that is on a good day, with a brand-new press. It is much more likely that the cyan will be ever so slightly out of register with the magenta, which in turn will be ever so slightly out of register with the yellow. The problem is that if you use a drawing program to create an image like the one shown in fig. 9.1, then the hole knocked out of the cyan square is exactly the same size and shape as the magenta circle that is doing the knocking. Given even a small amount of misregistration, the magenta element is almost certain to print with a slight overlap onto the cyan along one side, thus leaving a thin, crescent-shaped white space along the other.

The way to avoid this problem is to produce a very slight overlap between the magenta and cyan shapes. The area both colours then share is known as a trap.

It is not always possible to apply a trap in the way you might want. For example, in this case, if you were using Illustrator or CorelDRAW, it would be difficult to trap (i.e. expand) the cyan into the magenta. It could be done, but it would involve much more work. It would be easy, on the other hand, to trap the magenta into the cyan, simply by adding an outline and setting it to overprint. The thing to remember with traps is that it is always best to trap the lighter colour into the darker, and not the other way round. If the darker colour expanded into the lighter to create the trap, the result would compromise the shape of the lighter-coloured object. A good way to remember which way round to do this is to imagine the effect, both ways, for yellow type on a black background. Then you will remember that the only thing to do is to trap the yellow into the black, because that option leaves the shape of the type unchanged.

If the overlapping area is small enough, you will not see it. The juxtaposition of two bright colours, especially if they are close to being opposites, slightly dazzles the eye. Thus you would not notice even quite a large overlap (much more than you would want to apply as a trap) because the interaction between the colours, together with the after-image they produce on your retina, would cause you to see a slight optical illusion along their common edge that would make it difficult to see – even if no trap was applied. Alternatively, if the colours are not as bright as my example, or as contrasting, you are not going to see the trap between them simply because they are not bright or contrasting. When you look at an image, you are probably not really looking at detail. It is much more likely that at first you are just getting an overall impression. Maybe then you look a bit closer at the individual elements, but you tend not to investigate the edges where different elements touch, so long as the trap is small enough. Why? Because it is convincing. However, that only works if the trap is small enough to do the job it is intended to do, and not if it is so big that you can easily see it. So, obviously, the amount by which two colours are set to overlap is important.

Adobe Illustrator

In Illustrator there are two ways to deal with trapping. One is automatic, one is manual. To create a trap manually, add an outline of 0.25pt to an object and set it to overprint. You can do this by opening the Attributes palette and checking Overprint Stroke while the object is selected. To automate trapping between selected objects, use the Pathfinder palette. Select Trap and enter a width. Again, you will usually want 0.25pt. You can also specify a tint value to reduce the percentage of the lighter colour being trapped, which will make it even less visible.

CorelDRAW

In CorelDRAW, you can also create manual traps between objects by adding a thin outline and setting it to overprint. Select the object, add the outline, then right-click on it and choose Overprint Outline. While saving or exporting the file, make sure you have

trapping set to 'Preserve the document overprint settings' (you will find this option if you click on the Advanced button in the Export window), otherwise the trapping information will get left behind. This will also be the case if you try to export it as a TIFF. To create automatic traps, you will need to export the drawing as an EPS file. During this process you can click on the Advanced tab and choose Auto-spreading. The Maximum command lets you specify the width of the resulting trap.

Incidentally, when using Illustrator or CorelDRAW it is also useful to apply Overprint Fill to anything black that runs over an object of another colour. As black is the only colour that can overlay other colours without creating a visible mix, there is no need to knock out the image beneath it. Therefore, simply allowing it to overprint avoids the need for a trap. The page-layout programs generally allow black to overprint as a default.

Photoshop, InDesign and Quark

First, I should mention that you do not need to apply a trap to photographic images in Photoshop. Trap settings should only be used if you are creating a non-photographic type of image in which there are areas of adjacent flat or graduated colours that will be printed by different ink units on a press.

If you do want to apply a trap in Photoshop, read on.

The default setting is a 1-pixel trap, but of course the size of the pixels is up to you. A 1-pixel trap on a 300dpi image is ideal for most work. Choose Image > Trap, enter a pixel count of '1' and click OK. A 1-pixel trap on a 300dpi image will not really be noticeable, even when using it between two colours like cyan and magenta, whereas the alternative – a thin white crescent down one side of the magenta circle – would be very noticeable indeed.

Adobe InDesign's default trap setting is 0.25pt. InDesign also allows trapping for rich blacks, which is a very sophisticated extra (see 'Creating and Using a Rich Black', opposite). In Quark, however, the default trap amount is 0.144pt. Now, if a point is $\frac{1}{72}$ in, then 0.144 of a point is roughly $\frac{1}{500}$ in. If you ask your printers if they can hold registration throughout a four-colour run to $\frac{1}{500}$ in (or just over 0.05mm), they will probably laugh. To change the default trap settings in Quark, first ensure that no project is currently open (or the new settings will only apply to it) and choose (PC) Edit > (or Mac) QuarkXPress > Preferences > Default Print Layout > Trapping (fig. **9.2**). The 'Absolute' option assigns the given trap amount everywhere it is needed, whereas 'Proportional' will alter the amount of trapping depending on the lightness of the colour. I suggest setting process trapping to 'on' and increasing the default amount to 0.25pt. That increases the trap to $\frac{1}{288}$ in – the same as InDesign, and roughly the same as a 1-pixel trap on a 300dpi image.

In fig. **9.3** I have created three images with a background of solid cyan and a magenta circle in the middle. On the left, it has been generated by Adobe Illustrator and exported as an EPS file with a 1-pt trap. The centre image shows the same EPS file but with a 0.25-pt trap. On the right, the same image elements were created in Photoshop as a 300dpi TIFF file with a 1-pixel trap. (Incidentally, the file size for these images was only 220kb for the vector EPS files, but nearly 1.35MB for the TIFF, so that is clearly one area where vector EPS has an advantage. Of course, given current computer storage capacities it is not such a big deal as it used to be.)

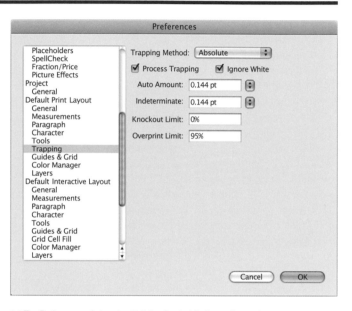

9.2 The Preferences window, in which the Quark default trapping settings can be changed.

9.3 Left: Adobe Illustrator EPS, 1-pt trap. Centre: Adobe Illustrator EPS, 0.25-pt trap. Right: Photoshop 300dpi image, 1-pixel trap.

Creating and Using a Rich Black

In the page-layout programs, black is usually set to overprint everything. That makes sense, because black is intended to be opaque and is never trying to create a third colour when it overlaps another. Pantone colours are also intended to be opaque although in practice they are not. However, cyan, magenta or yellow are intended to be transparent and thus create additional colour blends between them when one lands on top of another. Printing other elements within a large, solid-black background can be fraught with problems. For a start, in order to get a nice solid black, the printer cannot stint on the ink flow. Also, as it is most likely printing onto white paper, there has got to be enough ink, evenly spread, if it is going to look even and dense and not patchy. However, if there is a little bit too much ink, set-off might easily occur and ruin the job. This is where the ink on one sheet transfers to the – as yet – unprinted side of the sheet that lands on top of it in the pile after they have both gone through the press. Both of these results are definitely to be avoided.

To complicate matters further, if you have an image in the middle of the solid black area, then you are creating different ink requirements across your page. This might mean visible streaks unless the coverage is heavy enough to blot them out.

The example shown in fig. **9.4** shows the sort of thing that might happen. (The arrow indicates the direction of travel through the press.) On either side of the small four-colour image on the front cover of the piece (the upper right quarter of the sheet) there is a 100% requirement for black ink, but above and below the area occupied by the image it is closer to 80%. It is therefore quite likely that there will be a visible difference between the black solid in this area and the black solid on either side. The same is true of the lines of type and the small magenta squares, although to a much lesser degree.

The printer is left in a difficult position: either increase the ink flow and risk set-off, or leave the ink flow at a safer, lower level and maybe end up with visible streaks. A good way to avoid this problem is by creating a colour called a 'four-colour black' or 'rich black' using whichever of the major drawing, image-adjustment or page-layout programs you are using to create the front cover. A 'rich black' is a colour made up of 100% solid black combined with a supporting tint underneath it. This gives the black the extra density it needs without increasing the flow of ink to a possibly dangerous level.

For a 'rich black' I usually use a 40% tint of cyan plus 100% black (fig. **9.5**). For a four-colour black, I use a combination of a 30% tint of cyan, magenta and yellow together with a 100% black (fig. **9.6**). The three colours combine at (almost) equal

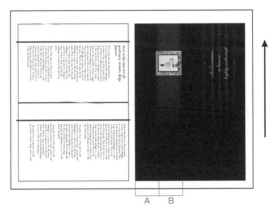

9.4 There is a different requirement for black ink between sections A and B, which could result in streaking if not enough ink is applied, or set-off if too much is applied.

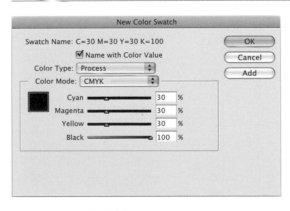

9.5 The New Colour Swatch window showing CMYK values for a 'rich black'…

9.6 …and also the values for a four-colour black.

densities to produce a neutral grey, and the printed result is an even, dense black with no visible pinholes. (There might actually be pinholes, but if there is a roughly 30% tint of grey underneath them, they are almost impossible to spot.) This means less stoppage time on the press, faster turnaround on the job, less quality control further down the production line and, best of all, the potential problems of set-off or a streaky print are avoided. If you create your own rich black, make sure you do not overload the maximum ink density, which has already been discussed (see previous page).

Some designers prefer to create a more dense black by adding only a 40% cyan, with no yellow or magenta. This makes a good solid black that has a somewhat cool appearance. On the other hand, adding only a 40% magenta – with no cyan or yellow – adds the appearance of red highlights. The effect is quite subtle, but as the addition of another tint enables the printer to lower the density of the black, the colour underneath can influence the overall appearance.

The best way to make these useful colours available to you is to add them to InDesign or Quark when you have no documents open. Then, any changes you make become program, rather than document, defaults. That means that once added, they will be there for any future documents you create. Of course, you will still need to add them where needed to documents that were created previously. To do this in InDesign, open the Swatches window. The default red, green and blue swatches are really of

9.7 The default Swatches window in InDesign.
9.8 (Bottom) The InDesign Swatches window after adding the rich and four-colour black swatches.

9.9 The Edit > Colours window in Quark.
9.10 (Bottom) The default Colours window in Quark.

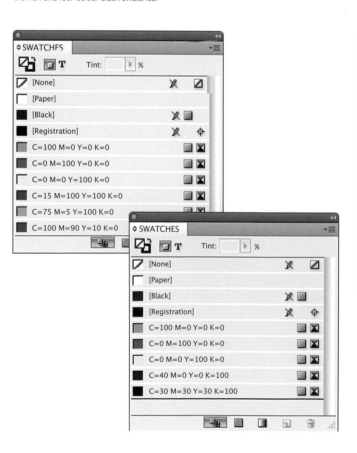

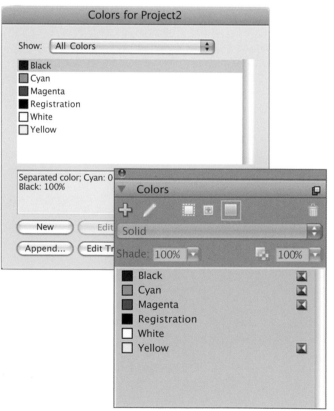

no use as they are simply the CMYK versions of the RGB colours (fig. **9.7**). If you needed a blue, for example, you would mix the blue you wanted rather than just using the one provided. So, delete these three (select them, then click on the Trash can at the foot of the window). Then, create the swatches for a four-colour black and a rich black, as already described. Your new Swatches window will look like this (fig. **9.8**).

In Quark the process is similar, but you would choose Edit > Colours to create the new swatches (fig. **9.9**). Incidentally, Quark included true RGB red, green and blue swatches as a default for many years before deciding that as they were downright dangerous in a project that would be printed, they should go (fig. **9.10**). Click on the New button to open the

Edit Colour window in which the new swatches can be created. After creating the swatch for a rich black (fig. **9.11**), click OK to return to the Colours window, where you can again click on New to create the four-colour black swatch (fig. **9.12**). When you have finished and return again to the Colours window, click Save to add them to the Colours window (fig. **9.13**).

9.11 The Edit Colour window showing values for a rich black…
9.12 …and for a four-colour black.

9.13 The Quark Colours window, after adding the rich and four-colour black swatches.

Registration and Trim Marks

The only places where the combined ink density should add up to more than the danger zone – in fact, it should add up to 400% – is in the trim marks and registration targets (fig. **9.14**) that are placed outside the 'live' area of the page and are therefore destined to be cut off and thrown away. The printer can use them to help register the job, and the binding department can use the trim marks to cut and fold it.

These marks can be added during the creation of a PDF file, or by the imagesetter when it prints the plates from a native file (e.g. an InDesign or Quark file rather than a PDF). It is also easy to add them yourself if you are designing something smaller than an A4 page that is going to be printed on its own – a custom shape, for example, or a matrix of business cards – but they will be of no use around the edge of an advertisement that will be dropped onto a larger layout, as any marks you add will just be cut off. You can easily create your own vector registration mark in Illustrator and save it as a small four-colour EPS file. You can also create the same thing as a 1200dpi black-and-white bitmap image in Photoshop, which can be coloured by specifying it as 'registration' (which is made up of all four process colours at 100%) in page-layout programs. You can also use the Scripts settings in InDesign to create them, which can then be copied and pasted to where they are needed. For trim marks, just draw a 0.5pt line, again specified as being 'registration' colour. If you want it to indicate a fold, use a dotted line instead, but write 'fold' next to it, so it is the printer's fault if they cut along it by mistake!

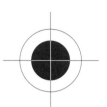

9.14 A printer's registration 'target'.

Trapping
into a Rich Black

9.15 Due to misregistration, the other colours present in the rich black can be seen around the edges of the white lettering.

9.16 The result when the cyan, magenta and yellow all hold a 'spread' image of the type, which has been expanded (hence 'spread') so that its shape is pushed away from the edges of the type shown in the black plate. This is known as a 'hold-back' setting.

The greatest difficulty arising from the use of a rich black is in trapping with other elements. As an example, imagine a brochure that has a solid black cover with a line of white type running across it. If a rich black is used, there will be a registration problem around the edge of the white type. It will probably have a thin cyan line visible along one edge, and perhaps magenta visible along another, and a faint hint of yellow on yet another.

Fig. **9.15** shows a scenario that is very common. However, there are ways of getting around this situation. For users of Quark, Illustrator and CorelDRAW, the solution is one that printers do not like and will try to dissuade you from using. Try not to be put off. I have used the following method more times than I can remember, and it has never yet failed. The idea is to send the printer two copies of the final file. From file 1, tell the printer to only run the black film (or plate if using CTP). The second version is an exact copy of the first with one exception: a white outline has been added to the type, thereby forcing all four colours away from it. Tell the printer to run only the cyan, magenta and yellow films (or plates) from this file.

As long as the printer does not run the black film (or plate) on Monday and then wait until the following Friday to run the other three colours – which could mean that the images on the two sets will not match perfectly because of various environmental differences – then the chances of their not fitting are no more than when running all the separations from a single file.

However, that is unlikely to prevent your printer from predicting dire consequences. It is quite likely that they will not have been asked to do this before, and one thing printers really dislike is a nasty surprise coming off the end of the press, especially if they might be held liable. Nevertheless, if you manage to persuade them to go ahead, the results will probably be one of the nicest things they ever printed. As a result, your standing with them will probably rise to such a point that you will get the red-carpet treatment from them from that time forth.

NB You can still use a digital proof when using this method, because you can run it from the first of the two files. Even though it is not exactly the configuration that will run on the press, none of the colour values will be any different.

The method described above has been used to create fig. **9.16**, which is a CMYK image using a rich black in which '1234567890' has had a white outline added in the magenta, cyan and yellow components.

In Illustrator and CorelDRAW, this is quite easy to do. In Quark, it is rather more difficult because you cannot add white outlines to type until it has been converted into a graphic image. To do this, highlight the text with the Text Content tool, or select it with the Item tool, and then choose Item > Convert Text to Box > Convert Entire Box. Then use the Colours window to apply white as the outline colour, and specify the outline width using Item > Frame. The second and third copies of the file are then sent to the printer, the second file being used to generate only the black and the third to generate the C, M and Y.

Because the black is reasonably opaque, no one will notice that right around the edge of the type there is an area that is not quite as dense as the rest of the background. For one thing, it is a very thin area. For another, there is a high degree of visible contrast. The eye will be slightly dazzled by the brightness of the type against the dark background, and so it will not see the tiny 'trap' area.

For users of InDesign, the news regarding rich black is very good. InDesign contains a trapping engine that allows the user to specify the width of a 'hold-back' setting, or to simply use the default as is. This keeps the supporting screens of the other colours away from the edges of reversed or light elements, so that they retain their sharpness in the final print. In other words, it traps a rich black perfectly.

Using Pantone Colours

10

As well as RGB and CMYK there is another colour system that you are likely to encounter in the world of print: the Pantone range. These can be used as an extension of the possibilities for someone without the budget, or the need, to print using the four-colour process, but who wants something more exciting than just a single colour. The swatch book covering the 'Pantone Solid Coated/Uncoated' range allows the viewer to see how each one of several thousand colours, each of which can be accurately mixed to a given formula, will print on coated and uncoated white stock. Printers will often offer to mix the ink themselves (cheaper but less accurate) or to buy it pre-mixed (accurate, but more expensive).

Pantone colours are also used in other situations – for instance, logo designs – which then need to be converted to their closest CMYK equivalents in order to keep printing costs down. Knowing how to do this is extremely useful, and knowing about the limitations of this conversion process will enable you to avoid expensive and unnecessary problems with your clients.

Opposite: The Pantone guides are very useful – and quite expensive. This one allows you to tear off a colour chip and keep it with the job from production to print.

The Pantone
Formula Guides

10.1 The Pantone Formula Guide books, on coated and uncoated stock.

Most designers who have sent their work to print shops have, at one time or another, run across Pantone colours. These are colours that printers can mix using the formula written under each sample in the swatch book (fig. **10.1**).

While the formula is designed to give the same result every time, there are inevitably slight variations between one mix and another. Therefore, if you plan on using the same colour repeatedly over time and want a high degree of consistency throughout, you may want to talk to the printer about mixing up a large batch and storing it for you for future use. You will save on mixing charges, and consistency will be improved, especially if you request that density readings are taken and matched to approved samples each time the colour is run.

The Pantone range can be mixed from a range of several 'standard' colours that come straight out of a can. These include not only the four process colours but also colours such as Pantone Green, Pantone Purple, Pantone Orange, Rubine Red and Reflex Blue. Therefore, the range of colours it is possible to mix goes way beyond a range limited to combinations of just C, M, Y and K.

Thus, when you are trying to match a Pantone colour using CMYK inks, you are likely to run into the same problem as when starting with an RGB colour: you cannot do it.

Pantone colours are, however, ideal for two-colour work and duotones. As I mentioned before, if you do not have a swatch book yourself – and they are quite expensive – your local print shop probably will. As well as making them available for client use, they probably upgrade them from time to time, and if so they might be persuaded to sell (or give) you the old ones. Despite dire warnings from the manufacturers, it takes several years for the colours to fade even slightly, especially if you keep them in a dark drawer somewhere. Just to be sure, check any older books you are planning on using against a new one.

Most of the difficulties I have run into concerning the use of Pantone colours fall within one of the following three scenarios.

Typical scenario 1

Problem: The clients use a particular Pantone colour for their logo. Now they want a four-colour brochure/ad/newsletter, but they do not want to go to the additional expense of running a fifth colour. So, the Pantone shade has to be converted to CMYK. Of course, when it does not convert accurately, it is your fault.

Solution: Educate your clients beforehand. Explain to them that the limitations of CMYK mean there is no easy way around this problem. Either they have to accept the change in colour, or they have to pay for the additional Pantone print run. It is their choice.

Typical scenario 2

Problem: The clients understand the problems associated with converting a Pantone colour to CMYK, and have decided to go for the fifth colour on the print run. How can you give them an accurate proof that shows them their Pantone colour?

Solution: Two choices.
First, you can run a reasonably pleasing digital proof or a Cromalin in which the Pantone colour defaults to the closest CMYK equivalent, and then reassure the clients that on the actual print run the printer will use the actual Pantone shade. If the job is a sure thing, you could also ask the printer to mix the colour for you (alternatively, if you want to be sure that the colour is accurate, ask them to buy it, pre-mixed) and do a **dab test** on a paper sample that can be shown to the clients for approval. You should only have to go through this once or twice before they trust you for all their future work.

The second choice is to use wet proofs. These are the most accurate kind of proof you can get as they are run on a real printing press using the same plates that your printer will use to run the job. They can even be printed on the same kind of paper you are going to print on, and they can use real Pantone ink mixes. However, you should bear in mind that wet proofs are also the most costly kind of proof available.

Typical scenario 3

Problem: The clients have decided to go for the fifth colour on the print run. But, they want the Pantone area to overlap a CMYK image.

Solution: There are two subcategories for this one.
If the Pantone colour is a solid, not a tint, things are fairly straightforward. There will not be a moiré problem because there are no additional screens involved, so the only thing to consider is the relative opacity of the inks and whether they should therefore be printed in a particular order.

Pantone colours are intended to be opaque rather than transparent, but they are not truly opaque. If you print them over the top of a CMYK image, those inks will still show through, though not as clearly as if the Pantone colour had been printed underneath them.

If the Pantone ink needs to appear to be completely opaque across a CMYK image, then the shape of the Pantone image has to be knocked out of the other channels. But first, a fifth channel has to be added to the other four that can hold the Pantone information.

To create this, open the image in Photoshop (fig. **10.2**). Then choose Window > Channels to open the Channels window. Click on the Options button at the top right of the window and select New Spot Channel (fig. **10.3**). Do not worry about giving

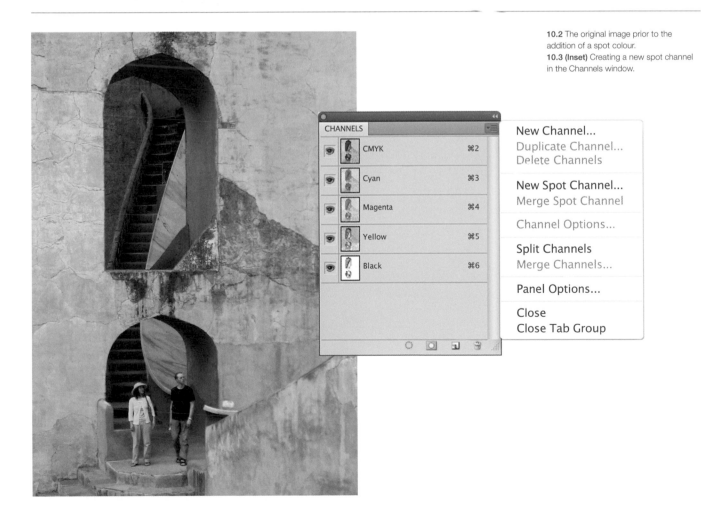

10.2 The original image prior to the addition of a spot colour.
10.3 **(Inset)** Creating a new spot channel in the Channels window.

the new spot channel a name, as Photoshop will do that automatically when you pick the colour you want. In the Ink Characteristics section, click on the coloured square (where it says Colour, as in fig. **10.4**) to open the Colour Picker window, then click on Colour Libraries to open the window in which you can specify a Pantone colour. You can simply type in the number if you do not want to scroll through the whole list. In this case I chose Pantone 199, a shade of red (fig. **10.5**). When you have selected the colour, click on OK to return to the Spot Channel window. The new channel appears, with the correct channel name (fig. **10.6**).

Incidentally, the Solidity percentage you can specify in the Spot Channel window is most useful when set to zero, as it will allow the rest of the CMYK image to show through. If you set it to 100% – i.e. completely opaque – you might believe that your Pantone colour will completely obscure the image beneath it. Not so. It is a setting that only affects the visual appearance on screen.

You will notice that while you have a single channel active, the foreground and background colours revert to shades of grey; this is also the case with your new spot channel.

Now you can paint, or copy and paste, the image that you want to print as a Pantone colour into the spot colour channel. When you make the composite channel at the top of the channels 'pile' active again, you will see the result. (Of course, what you will actually be looking at is an RGB representation of a CMYK image with an RGB representation of a Pantone colour overlaying it!)

10.4 The New Spot Channel window in which a specific colour, from a specific library, is chosen for the new channel.
10.5 (Bottom) Type the colour number on the keyboard and it is selected in the Colour Libraries window.

10.6 (Inset) The new spot channel in the Channels window.
10.7 The type is added to the image, on a second layer.

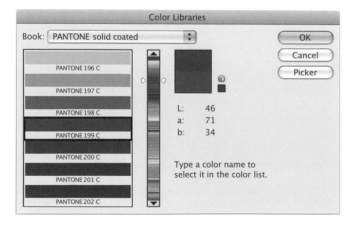

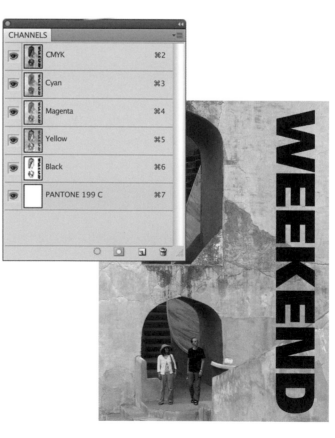

First generate the image you want. In this example, I have used the word 'Weekend' in bold type on a new layer (fig. **10.7**); its shape can be selected by clicking on the thumbnail image in the type layer while holding down the Control or Apple key.

Then make the Pantone channel active by clicking on it (which makes the selection of the type apply to that channel); set black as the foreground colour (**Note:** if you wanted to use a tint rather than a solid colour you would choose that percentage of grey instead); and choose Alt + Backspace to fill that shape, on the Pantone channel, with solid colour. In the channel, the shape of the type appears in solid black (fig. **10.8**), but as that channel controls a Pantone colour, it appears in the image as solid red 199 (fig. **10.9**).

If you want to avoid having the CMYK areas print underneath the solid Pantone colour, you will need to create a selection of the spot-channel image and knock it out of the other four channels in a way that allows the Pantone colour to trap into the others. To do this, and while you still have the shape active as a selection, choose Select > Modify > Contract and enter a value of 1 pixel. Then choose the other channels one by one and delete the information within the selected area. This ensures a small trap between the CMYK and the Pantone colours (fig. **10.10**).

If the Pantone colour is a tint, not a solid, then further complications arise. This is because there are no more available screen angles for another colour. As we have seen (see Chapter 2), there are not actually enough screen angles for the CMYK

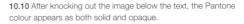

10.8 (Inset) With the new spot channel selected in the Channels window, a selection of the type is filled with black.
10.9 Filling the text area with black means, on the spot channel, that it is filled with solid Pantone colour.

10.10 After knocking out the image below the text, the Pantone colour appears as both solid and opaque.

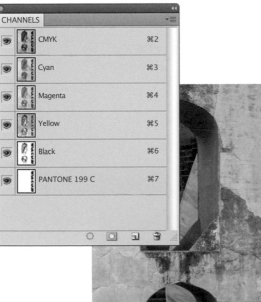

colours, and they only work together without producing a visible moiré pattern because of the unusual visual properties of yellow (you can see its colour, but you cannot see its shape).

The solution here is again to generate a selection based on the spot channel (and again reduce that selection by 1 pixel to create a trap) and then knock it out of either the cyan, magenta or black channels. Then you can tell the printer to run the Pantone tint at the same screen angle as the colour you have knocked out. The reason you cannot do this in the yellow channel is, of course, because printing your Pantone colour at the yellow screen angle will produce a visible moiré. Only colours like process yellow are able to produce moiré patterns that we cannot actually see.

Regardless of whether the Pantone colour is a solid or a tint, you will need to save the result as either a DCS2 (desktop colour separation 2) image, or a PSD file. In the first case, as DCS2 is actually an EPS format, you will be prompted to choose the image header type. For the best screen image, choose an 8-bits-per-pixel TIFF preview (which will be made up of 256 colours) and DCS with Colour Composite (72 pixels/inch). PC users should save with the ASCII option, Mac users with Binary (fig. **10.11**). However, if you choose to save the result as a PSD, you won't need to do anything further.

Then, when you import the result into InDesign or Quark, you will see a colour image that includes the Pantone channel, and the Pantone colour (which will have automatically been added to the Swatches window) will be able to carry through to the PDF and generate a separate plate (or film) in addition to those required for the CMYK components.

NB If you are sending files to your printer in PDF format, the whole file, including any DCS2 and PSD images in the layout, can be checked in Adobe Acrobat by clicking on Advanced > Print Production > Output Preview. In the top part of that window the four CMYK colours are listed, below which are additional Pantone colours (fig. 10.12). Each can be unchecked to remove that colour from the preview, allowing you to check that, for example, the black type really is black rather than a combination of C, M, Y and K.

Incidentally, when asking a printer for a price on a job that uses one of the Pantone standard colours (the ones that come straight out of the can), remember to mention that there should not be any mixing charge added for the Pantone colour. It always helps to let printers know that *you* know what you are talking about.

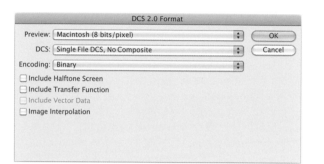

10.11 The DCS2 Format window in which the characteristics of the preview image are set.

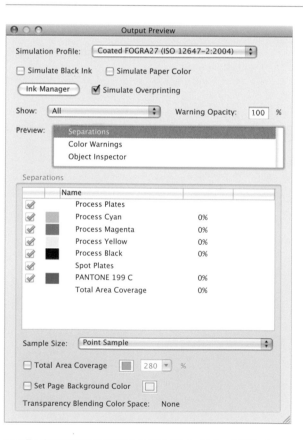

10.12 The Output Preview window in Acrobat showing the four CMYK colours plus the Pantone.

Other Pantone Products

While the Pantone Matching System guide is probably the most commonly encountered member of the Pantone range, there are several other swatch books that will be of enormous help to graphic designers. To see them all, visit www.pantone.com.

The metallic formula guide

The Pantone Metallic Coated range is much smaller than the Solid Coated range. It provides a beautiful and exotic set of mixes between straight-out-of-the-can metallic inks and PMS colours, and the results on-press can be amazing. However, the ability of metallic inks to be reflective – and there is not much point in using a metallic ink if it is not allowed to be reflective – relies on a hard, smooth, coated paper surface. You cannot expect to get the same results from an uncoated stock, especially if it also has a textured finish. Some kinds of varnish have a detrimental effect on the metallic appearance, but fortunately the swatch book offers both varnished and unvarnished samples of each colour. However, it is also possible to use a varnish to increase the effectiveness of a metallic ink by first printing it onto those areas that will then be overprinted with the metallic. To be most effective, the varnish should be a 'spot' rather than a 'flood' application, so that it only underprints the metallic area and not the entire sheet. The varnish will then help to seal the sheet, allowing the metallic to be more reflective, while not changing the appearance of the paper surface elsewhere.

Pantone metallic shades are much closer to being completely opaque than Pantone colours, simply because of the opacity of the metallic element.

Obviously there are many other intermediate mixes that can be extrapolated from the formulas given in the swatch book. If your clients want a shade that is not represented, it should not be too hard to come up with a mix that lands between the two swatches closest to the desired colour. Just make sure they agree beforehand that the responsibility for heading into such uncharted territory is theirs, and not yours!

The pastel formula guide

This range is even smaller than the metallic guide. Each pastel colour swatch has two tear-out chips. Pantone has developed a base palette specifically for this pastel range in order to make it easier for printers consistently to mix accurate pastel colours with a minimum of waste.

The four-colour process guide

This contains many colour swatches made up from the four 'process' inks, i.e. C, M, Y and K, and is available in both coated and uncoated formats. It is extremely helpful in figuring out the accuracy of on-screen colours as well as being an invaluable aid to deciding which tints to use in a layout. If you ever need to choose a CMYK colour, this book is absolutely the best way to do it.

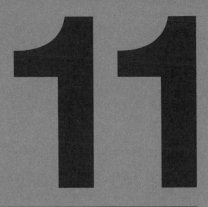

Photoshop Tips and More

Adobe Photoshop is my favourite graphics program of all time. Even though I have been using it for years and years, and even though I am an Adobe Certified Expert (ACE) in Photoshop and regularly teach both introductory and advanced courses, I constantly run into new ways of doing things, or just new things.

No matter what the problem is with an image, it seems that it can be fixed with one or more of the astounding range of tools in Photoshop. Usually the only additional things the user will need are time and patience, neither of which Adobe can supply.

Despite this vast potential, most people just use the areas they feel comfortable with and do not explore further – and this is a great shame. Whatever your level of experience, adding a new method here and there will gradually allow you to achieve results that you previously considered to be beyond your abilities. And, if you keep at it, pretty soon you will be able to do things that you used to think were downright impossible.

With that in mind, here are a few tips and tricks to help you make some adjustments that you probably thought were beyond you. As you will see, they are not.

Opposite: Where would graphic designers be without an edge – hints and tips that enable them to do particular things that other designers can't? Here are a few that may come in handy.

11.1 The original skateboarder image.

11.2 The original image, plus a second layer filled with the specified colour and set to a layer blending mode of Hue. The colour has been erased from the areas in which it was not wanted.

11.3 Another colour variation created on a third layer in the same image.

Changing an Object's Colour

I almost did not write this chapter, as there are already many excellent books that can show you how to do incredible things with Photoshop. However, there are a few methods that I have found to be extremely useful but I have rarely, if ever, seen mentioned in any of the books I have read, so I thought it would be worthwhile to include one or two of them here.

Most Photoshop users will have already experimented with adjusting the colour of an object using various methods, but in general these are somewhat hit-and-miss. There is, however, a less well-known method that allows you to accurately change the colour of an object while preserving all the highlight and shadow information at the same time.

Let us take as an example an image of an air-borne skateboarder. As you can see, his shirt is red (fig. **11.1**).

How about if you wanted to make it a different colour? And you could be very specific here, choosing an exact CMYK tint. Set it as the foreground colour, then open the Layers window and create a new transparent layer. Fill it with the new foreground colour (Alt + Backspace), and then select Hue as the blending mode (fig. **11.2**) from the drop-down list in the Layers window.

The shirt will change colour, while preserving the shadows and highlights. So, unfortunately, will everything else that had a discernible hue – but if something was a neutral colour beforehand, it still is now, as this blending mode only affects things which were a discernable colour. If they were neutral, they remain unchanged.

You can also use Colour as the blending mode, which colours everything in the image. Colour mode also tends to give less contrast between shadows and highlights.

Of course, you could create a selection of the areas you wished to change before applying the colour and blending mode. Otherwise, you will now need to use either the Eraser tool, a selection or a mask to delete the new colour from the areas in which it is not needed. If you accidentally erase the new colour from an area where it was wanted, simply paint it back in using the Paintbrush tool with an Opacity and Hardness of 100%. When you are happy with the result, flatten the layers and save. To see another colour, repeat the operation on another new layer (fig. **11.3**). You can create as many variations as you want in a single image.

The advantage of using this method over other colouring options is that you can specify an exact tint that is then the basis for the entire tonal range of the object.

Smooth Gradients

The Gradient tool in Photoshop is one of my all-time favourite painting tools. Prior to digital methods, creating a gradient required all kinds of messing around in a darkroom. First, you needed either an airbrushed piece of artwork – and it was not easy (or cheap) to get one painted with a really smooth gradient – or you had to create one photographically by using lights and an angled backdrop, usually a huge roll of paper several metres wide. Either way, the result had to replace the existing background in the photo in question, which meant painting a mask (with no possibility of anti-aliasing) and making double exposures onto yet another piece of film. At every stage of the process great care had to be taken to ensure that the highlights did not burn out, nor the shadows burn in. It was all very complicated. This was territory only ventured into by the qualified or the foolish, and only the qualified emerged with a usable result.

In Photoshop it is all much easier. Isolate your object by selecting and deleting unwanted areas, then decide on your foreground and background colours. Create a new layer, place it behind the original and click and drag the cursor across it to determine the start and end points for your gradient.

But there are still a couple of things that it is useful to know. Unless you take care to avoid it, you can end up with visible 'banding' across the tinted area. This is typically caused by, for example, filling an area with a very subtle tint that only contains a small number of shades of a colour. The way to avoid it is by adding 'noise' to the layer containing the gradient. The noise filter acts a bit like an editable dither. It scatters the pixels around, and can easily create a 'sandblasted' effect if overapplied, because it also changes the hue and contrast levels of individual pixels. At full strength it produces a chaotic mass of primary and secondary colours. However, if it is used to dither the pixels very slightly, it simply removes visible banding and makes a gradient even smoother. I usually apply a setting of 3 if I am working with a 300dpi image. If you zoom in after applying it, close enough to see the individual pixels, you will see that your gradient has been jiggled around just a bit. Despite the apparently rougher appearance, it will now print smoother than before.

The other important thing to know is that, whenever possible, it is best to add gradients to images *after* changing the colour mode to CMYK. If you add them in RGB mode and then convert the image, they will not be as smooth.

Using Desaturation to Avoid RGB Problems

Fixing Foreshortening

One day you will probably find yourself faced with having to use an image that has not only been provided by the client in RGB mode but is filled with what are obviously bright RGB colours.

If you try changing the mode to CMYK, all these RGB colours will immediately become their 'closest' CMYK equivalent, which might, of course, not look anything like the original. That is because in order to find the appropriate CMYK colour, Photoshop simply reverses the polarity of the percentages of RGB and renders those values as the new CMY(K) shade. So, if the RGB colour was made up of red and green completely off and blue completely on, it becomes instead a CMY colour made up of C and M (almost) completely on and Y completely off. The result is that on screen the colour turns from being an intense, glowing blue to being a dark, bluish-purple. Nevertheless, as far as Photoshop is concerned, it has done a good job with the conversion.

If your image contains a mix of colours that are both inside and outside the CMYK range, and only those colours outside it change when you convert the image, it can lead to a very unbalanced result.

To avoid this, do not make the colour-mode conversion immediately. While the image is still in RGB mode, choose Image > Adjustments > Hue & Saturation, and then gently reduce the saturation level. As you do so, you are pulling all the RGB colours in the image back towards the CMYK range. The image is adjusted holistically because you are working on everything at once, and this means your image maintains the overall balance it had to begin with. Best of all, you get to decide where you want the process to stop, which is how you should approach all your image adjustments.

Any time you take a picture of tall objects they will appear to taper towards a very high central point. This is called foreshortening and can easily be fixed using a variation of Free Transform.

You can see the foreshortening effect in fig. **11.4**. Duplicate the layer using Control/Apple + J, then create a Free Transform frame with Control/Apple + T. Normally, you would only be able to transform the image as a rectangular shape, but if you hold down the Control or Apple key, the frame toggles into Distort mode, allowing you to click and drag on a corner handle. With an image such as this, dragging the top right corner slightly to the right and the top left corner slightly to the left straightens the image content (fig. **11.5**).

NB If you only want to desaturate certain ranges of colour in your image, try selecting them by using Select > Colour Range. This method can give much better and more convincing results than by using the Magic Wand tool.

11.4 Foreshortening makes tall objects taper towards a vanishing point.   **11.5** Foreshortening, fixed.

11.6 Top Left: The RGB image, showing all three component channels in transparent colour: Red, Blue and Green.
Top Right: The 'morning' version, i.e. the blue channel. **Bottom Left:** The 'midday' version, i.e. the green channel. **Bottom Right:** The 'evening' version, i.e. the red channel.

Useful Greyscale Options

If you need to generate a greyscale image from an RGB original, you might want to consider whether you want the morning, noon or evening version (fig. **11.6**).

This will not work with a CMYK image because the colour information is spread between the channels in a completely different way, but if you are starting with an RGB version of a picture taken outdoors, and especially if there is a blue sky in the image, it might work very well.

In the mornings, blue light tends to be strongest and most visible. That is why morning light tends to look cooler. Towards the middle of the day neither blue- nor red-light densities have the upper hand, so things even out. Then, as the sun goes down, red light becomes stronger. You can use this to your advantage by simply opening up the Channels window and clicking on the channels, one by one. As you do so, the image will appear as the greyscale image contained in that channel.

(If the channels do not appear in greyscale but in colour, go to Edit > Preferences > Interface and uncheck 'Show channels in colour' in the top left corner.)

When you have made your choice, keep that channel selected and delete the others. Their names will change because Photoshop will no longer know what to call them. When your selected channel is the only one left, convert the image into greyscale format (Image > Mode > Greyscale), calibrate it according to the printing method you need to use, and save.

Normally, when you try to convert a colour image to greyscale, Photoshop tries to steer you towards using Image > Adjustments > Black and White as the appropriate method (fig. 11.7). In that window, you can adjust individual colour ranges to brighter or darker shades of grey. It is a very good method, but it is quite easy to burn out detail, so be careful.

Because the calibration method described in Chapter 6 retains all the tone information in the image, it is possible to adjust the settings more than once. For example, if an image is needed for printing on coated stock, it could first be calibrated for that and subsequently recalibrated for an uncoated-paper press run at a later date.

11.7 The Black and White window allows you to lighten or darken a variety of colours as they are converted to greyscale.

Sharpening Images in Photoshop

Most users of Photoshop will have made use of the Sharpening filters from time to time. I have often met designers who prefer the presets of Sharpen and Sharpen More because they seem to do a reasonable job, whereas they have noticed that the use of Unsharp Mask tends to cause light or dark edges around things. Unfortunately, because our screens are more forgiving than the average printing press, if you see this effect even slightly on screen you can guarantee that it will appear much more pronounced in print. However, if it is used in the right way, Unsharp Mask is an extremely effective sharpening filter.

The reason why these edges appear is due to the way in which a sharpening filter works. Not surprisingly, Photoshop cannot actually sharpen an image so that you will see more detail than existed before. Instead, it searches for edges within the image and boosts the contrast level alongside them. The effect is as if we can suddenly see the detail more clearly. It is an illusion, but it can be very convincing.

Unsharp Mask is my main sharpening filter, primarily because it is editable. It therefore puts me in control of the level of adjustment that I want to make. Given that the printing press is going to accentuate whatever I do with the filter, I always take care not to sharpen to the point of clearly seeing those high-contrast edges. This is basically a matter of experience, and the only thing to do is to go carefully. However, there are a couple of other things that can help.

Unsharp Mask uses three different settings: Threshold, Radius and Amount (fig. **11.8**). The Threshold determines which colours within the image will be affected by the adjustment. A setting of 0 for levels means that everything will be sharpened. The Radius slider determines how far away from the edges the sharpening effect will spread. If you hold this to between 1 and 2 pixels, those high-contrast halos will be much smaller and therefore harder to see. Lastly, the Amount is the strength of the sharpening itself. Holding the Radius to a lower level enables a higher level of sharpening to be applied without running into problems.

Using these settings will immediately improve your results, but here is another very good method that can be used at the same time.

If you are applying the sharpening to the whole image, then all the colours in all the channels are being worked on simultaneously. However, the sharpness of an image relies much more on the relative lightness and darkness of tone than it does on the colour information. If the colours can be left out while the sharpening is done, they will not be included in any

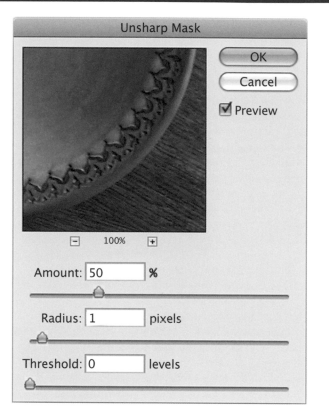

11.8 The Unsharp Mask window.

11.9 The channel components of an image in LAB mode: Lightness (top); A and B (bottom).

resulting distortion around edges within the image. This, too, will cut down on visible halos.

In order to do this, the image must first be converted into **LAB mode**. LAB is the widest colour space available, even slightly bigger than RGB. Therefore you can convert into LAB mode and back again without changing any colour data in your image, no matter where you start from. In other words, it is a 'safe' mode. The name 'LAB' comes from the names given to the three colour channels that make up a LAB image: Lightness, A and B. The lightness channel holds all the detail in the image in terms of light and shade. Channels A and B hold all the colour information. If you mess around with the A and B channels, you will park your image up a tree faster than you can believe, but for those who want to know, the A channel holds all the colour information for areas that contain red or green. Green shows up as darker-than-50% grey, red as lighter. Non-red and non-green areas show up as a neutral 50% grey. The B channel does the same thing for blue and yellow (fig. **11.9**).

By clicking on the Lightness channel in the Channels window, and then applying Unsharp Mask, you can apply sharpening to a much greater degree than would otherwise be possible. Then simply convert the image back into either RGB or CMYK (fig. **11.10**).

Fig. **11.11** shows two examples of the kind of distortion that sharpening in CMYK mode can lead to. Both have been oversharpened in order to make the differences between them easier to see. In the top image, all four CMYK channels were sharpened simultaneously using a Radius setting of 10 and an Amount setting of 200. In the bottom image, the same settings were used, but they were only applied to the Lightness channel while the image was in LAB mode. The contrast is the same in both images, but the additional colour distortion can clearly be seen in the top image.

Fig. **11.12** shows a much healthier image. Once again, sharpening was applied only to the Lightness channel in LAB mode, but this time with a Radius setting of 1 and an Amount of 200.

11.10 The original image in CMYK mode.

11.11 The image sharpened in CMYK mode with the Radius setting at 10 and the Amount at 200.

The image sharpened with a Radius setting of 10 and an Amount of 200, but only in the Lightness channel in LAB mode. This results in a similar increase in contrast but no distortion of colour values.

11.12 A Radius setting of 1 and an Amount of 200 applied to the Lightness channel in LAB mode.

11.13 (Below Left) The tint jump when using a round dot.

11.14 (Below Right) For an oval dot, the tint jump is divided into two smaller ranges.

11.15 (Bottom) A diamond dot does not create a tint jump until the darker shadow areas are reached, but then it fills in completely.

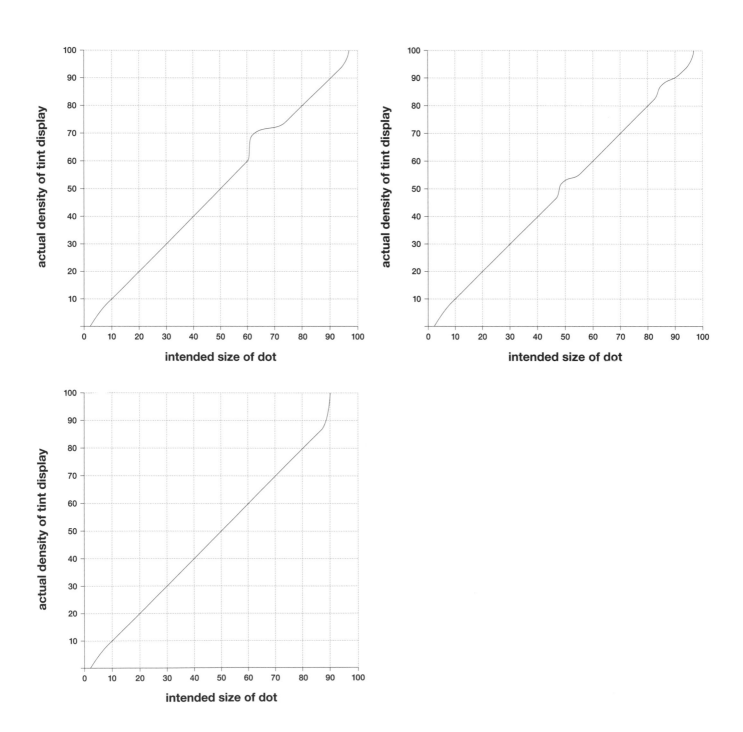

Choosing the Right Halftone Dot Shape

As you can see in fig. 11.12, the quality of the result when using Unsharp Mask depends very much on a low Radius setting and whether the colour within the image is included in the adjustment or left out.

Round dots are fine for almost every application, but there might be occasions when an oval, or perhaps a diamond dot, will produce a better print. The reason for this is because of what happens when two dots meet.

As dot size increases, the point at which they touch gets closer and closer. As this happens, the percentage of the tint increases. When they actually touch, they grab onto each other as if they were long-parted friends. This creates a **tint jump**, and several percentage points of tint value are lost as a result (fig. **11.13**).

If you are printing an image in which the middle-range colour values are particularly important – Caucasian flesh tones, for example – and you want to get as much out of the tint range as you possibly can, an oval dot would be a better choice than a round dot.

This is because the single tint jump that happens when using a round dot is divided into two smaller tint jumps when you use an oval dot. Round dots suddenly join up on four sides, but oval dots first collide at each end and then, further towards the shadows, they overlap at the top and bottom as well (fig. **11.14**).

The result is a small tint jump slightly to the highlight side of the mid-tones, and another small tint jump out towards the shadows. The area between these is where most of the flesh tones will print.

Diamond dots are actually square, but if we were using just one colour – black – we would set the screen at an angle of 45°, therefore all the squares would be tipped onto one corner (fig. **11.15**) – hence 'diamond'.

This shape allows completely even tone reproduction right up to around 90% density; then suddenly everything fills in completely. The dots join up not at single points but along whole sides. So, it is a very good shape to use for images that do not have any dense shadow areas.

Usually the dot shape is a feature of imagesetter printing rather than something to deal with yourself, so it is important to tell the printer where you want it applied.

Preparing the File for the Printer 12

The final step in the graphic design process is making sure that everything is ready for the printer. Oddly enough, this is when most mistakes happen. Why? Because things like colour mode, image formats, greyscale and colour calibration, colour management systems, the ability to create a good PDF in which everything necessary to successful printing is included, were not taken care of along the way. And of course, the list goes on. And all of these things create stress which you *do not need to go through*.

The wish to get away from the stress caused by 'not knowing how it is done' is, hopefully, why you bought this book in the first place. This chapter tells you how to check your work, and then how to adjust PDF presets for the specific requirements of the job. Creating a good PDF, like almost everything else we need to be able to do, is easy enough – as long as you know what you are doing.

Opposite: Ta-da! The final file, ready to roll – complete with colour bars, trims, registration marks and 'slug' information. And, of course, the content!

A Printing Checklist

When the final design has been approved by the client and all the production work has been completed, it is time to send the job out to the printer. This is when you will be really happy if you have done everything possible to prepare things for the press.

Obviously, most of the book so far has been intended to help you prepare things correctly. Even so, despite taking great care every step of the way, it is still alarmingly easy for mistakes to get through. From personal experience I can say that hitting File > Save for the last time does not mean it is now okay to relax. It is time for a clear head – and a detailed checklist.

The last thing you want is for an error to get through that everyone will blame on you. So, as well as checking your own work as far as possible, it is also important to communicate clearly with your printer so that there are no grey areas of responsibility that could come back to haunt you. This in turn means that anything you set up with the printer verbally should be backed up in writing. Remember, too, that a little more information than was needed is infinitely preferable to a little less than was needed.

Image checklist

If you are sending a printer a PDF file, you can skip ahead to 'Using Adobe Acrobat' on page 142. However, if you are sending a 'native' (InDesign, Quark, etc.) file that contains linked images, read on.

When you collect the material to send to the printer, then as well as the InDesign or Quark file you must also send the images – as separate items. These should be CMYK or greyscale TIFF, EPS (i.e. EPS or DCS2), PDF or PSD format. Nothing should be in RGB colour, and you should not have used any GIFs, JPEGs (if possible – and it is almost *always* possible), PNGs (Portable Network Graphics) or BMPs (windows bitmaps). The EPS format can also be used for Duotone (two colour channels; see page 83) images.

Check that all the images you are sending are the correct high-resolution versions, and not low-resolution 'for position only' (FPO) copies.

Delete all the alpha channels. These are additional channels that are sometimes added to images in order to save selections or create masks. If you leave them in place, they will confuse many imagesetters and generally cause problems. They are extremely useful tools for image creation, but do try to remember to remove them.

Avoid clipping paths, except where they are really needed. If you do need them, check that the pages in your document that contain such images print successfully on a PostScript printer *before* you send the job out. Clipping paths are vector rather than bitmap, so they cut right across pixels, and this can make the image look as if it has been cut out and pasted into place. PSD files support anti-aliased edges, which usually look much nicer.

Bleeds: images that need to run off the page should extend at least 3mm (⅛in) beyond the page boundaries, except on the binding edge (the 'inside' margin in InDesign), where they should end at the edge of the page.

Make sure that the written information accompanying the job lists all the images, whether linked or embedded, by their actual file names. If you are working on a PC, this will also indicate the format (.tif, .eps etc). If you are working on a Mac, you should also indicate which image file is in what format even if the file names themselves do not show the extensions.

Text checklist

Make sure, beforehand, that the printer has all the fonts needed to print the job.

Check that there are no 'surprise' fonts associated with the page-layout file, because, even if they do not actually format any of the text in your work, but only empty line spaces, it might hold things up while everyone tries to figure out what is happening. If blank line spaces are formatted with fonts that you did not intend to use, you should go through the job and change their specification to fonts that you *have* actually used. Otherwise the file will put up an error message as it is being opened, and this may delay everything while the printer tries to contact you to sort things out. If there is not time for you to do this, tell the printer to expect Arial (or whatever) to show up as a required font, but that it will not be a problem as it is only applied to blank line spaces. Therefore nothing will get through onto the plates (or film) except the leading value associated with that line of type, which will remain the same regardless of the font specification.

Make sure that all the required fonts are listed in the information you send with the job. Even though it is unlikely to be needed, also let the printer know the format (e.g. PostScript, TrueType, OpenType) of the fonts you have used.

General checklist

In your page-layout file, check that any graphics you have created are not stroked (outlined) or filled with RGB colours. Also, if you have added new swatches, make sure that they are specified as 'process' rather than 'spot' colours, otherwise they will output either as a separate sheet of film or an additional plate.

If the job includes a 'spot' varnish, i.e. a varnished area that is a distinct shape rather than a 'flood' varnish, which goes everywhere, it is a good idea to include the information in the form of an additional Pantone colour. Tell the printer, in writing, that the Pantone actually represents the varnish area and is not intended to print in the specified colour.

If you have run type across an image or a background colour, check that it is easily readable – remembering that it only takes a very tiny degree of frustration to make someone turn the page and go on to something else. The image that the text runs across should be ghosted back to around 20–25% of its original strength. Remember, you will be prepared to read it, but that is because you are the designer. Others will be less prepared to do so unless it is made *absolutely* easy.

Print out a complete copy of your job and send it with the digital files.

If the job requires folding, send an actual-size folding dummy, i.e. a full-size, folded model of the entire job. These are best if they are made using the same, or a very similar, paper stock to the one you will actually be using. In your file, cuts should be indicated by solid lines outside the live area, and folds should appear as dotted lines – and it does not hurt to type 'cut' or 'fold' (outside the live image area, of course) next to the appropriate line.

Folds are sometimes scored beforehand, especially if the stock is quite heavy and/or it is going to be folded against the grain. If you are using a fairly heavy paper but the printers have not spoken to you about scoring the job, it is possible that they have forgotten to factor this into their estimate. In this case you should ask them whether the folds will be against or with the grain on the press, and if that is likely to cause problems.

At the print shop

Things to do when getting an estimate for a job

If you have not used a particular print shop before, ask them to send you some *representative* samples of their work, well before you actually face a heavy deadline. 'Representative' means that you do not want to see only the best things they ever did, because they will not be indicative of the quality level you can fairly expect. You need to see samples of the kind of quality they produce every day.

Proofs

Decide what kind of proof you need. These days, I only use digital prints as proofs. This is partly because they are so cheap, and partly because they are also so accurate. A good digital printer can even emulate the CMS (colour-management system) that you have in place, so the result should be extremely close to what would come off a press.

Wet proofs, generated using CMYK inks and the actual plates that will be used to run the job, are also extremely accurate – but they are very expensive, especially when compared to digital prints.

The worst kind of proofs are pages that have been run from an in-house colour laser printer. These, while being the cheapest proofing option, can be so bad in terms of colour accuracy that they are misleading. In this case they are worse than useless and should only be used for basic positioning of the various elements, and to check for typographical errors.

Desktop inkjet machines are generally much more accurate in terms of colour but are rarely PostScript machines, meaning that EPS files in particular will not print very well. Also, as they can only translate RGB rather than CMYK images, they are really only of use during the design and layout production stages. Although I often use laser proofs as an aid during production, I never send these to the print shop as a representative proof.

Things to back up in writing

I always request that the printer (or repro house) should call me immediately if there are any problems. *Immediately*. If you do not get feedback in time, you may miss deadlines. Because this is so important to me, I stress this when talking to prospective printers, and make it very clear just how important it is to me. They should get the message that if they don't come through on this point I am very unlikely to return.

Make sure that the written information tells the printer the size of the job in terms of page dimensions and numbers, and

Using
InDesign

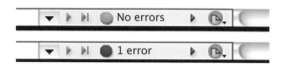

12.1 The Preflight button in InDesign, at the lower left corner of the screen. Click on it to show Preflight options.

how many ink colours are required. If you are using Pantone colours, list them by name. Ideally when ordering anything other than black-and-white work, you should send in a colour print of your file rather than a single-colour laser proof.

Check with your printer about trapping. This is particularly important if you are creating a high-resolution PDF file, which may be impossible to edit later on.

Quantity, paper stock, price and terms of delivery should be detailed on the written quote the printer has supplied to you. However, it is very common for a range of quantities and prices to have been given. Confirm in writing which options you have decided on *before* work begins.

Ask the printer to make sure that type has not reflowed before going to the trouble of running a proof. This is especially important if the proof relies on generating film. I once sent out the file for a 700-page book and forgot to mention this. The type reflowed – only a very small amount, it is true – but by the time it came to the end of chapter three, the last line could not fit on the page and instead jumped to the first page of chapter four. The rest of the film for the book was therefore scrap – for which I had to pay!

Is the job date-specific? If so, make sure the printers know that they cannot be late.

Confirm the number of copies you need to receive. If you require 1,000 invitations, tell the printer that you cannot accept less. Otherwise, it may be a shock when the printer delivers 900 and merely makes an adjustment to the bill. For more details on this, see 'Over- and under-runs' later in this chapter.

If your job includes the production of film that you or your client would like to keep, ask for it to be specified on the invoice. The plates are very unlikely to be of use to you as they can only be run on exactly the same machine; and, as they are also very easily damaged, it is not usually worth asking for them.

(For more information on these last two points, see 'Tools of the Trade, and More' on page 152.)

InDesign has a Preflight option in the lower left corner of the document window which enables you to check various aspects of the document before making a final PDF. A green button means everything governed by the current profile is OK, whereas a red button means the document has a problem (fig. **12.1**). However, the default preflight profile will not warn you about the inclusion of RGB images. As this is extremely useful, it is a good idea to create a new profile which *will* warn you.

To do this, click on the small grey arrow to the right of the green (or red) button and choose 'define profiles' from the list. Give the new profile the name 'colour warning', then click the arrow against 'colour'. Check the box next to 'colour spaces and modes not allowed', and then on the arrow beside it to open that area. Now, check the boxes against RGB, Lab and Spot Colour. Click Save then OK to close the window.

To apply your new profile, double-click on the red/green button to open the Preflight window and choose it from the list. It will then become the profile associated with that document. To apply your new profile as the default setting, click on the 'options' button in this window and choose 'preflight options'.

To create a PDF from an open (and preferably saved) document, choose File > Export. You are prompted to create a file name and choose a destination. When you click Save, the Export Adobe PDF window appears (fig. **12.2**).

At the top is a drop-down list of presets from which you should select the one most suited to the current purpose (fig. **12.3**). In the bottom left corner is the Save Preset button. This can be used to save and name an edited version of any of the presets, which will then be added to the drop-down list.

The main area of the window, on the right, displays the options for the item currently selected in the list on the left side, which has General at the top (as shown in fig. 12.2).

12.2 The Export Adobe PDF window.
12.3 (Bottom) The default list of PDF presets.

Making a low- or high-res
PDF from InDesign

General
These settings cover options such as the range of pages to include, whether to do so as spreads or single pages, interactive options and compatibility.

Low-res
If interactive materials *are* involved in your document, check Bookmarks, Hyperlinks and Interactive Elements. The 'Optimize for fast web view' and 'View PDF after exporting' boxes are checked as a default. If they remain checked, neither will be a problem regardless of the kind of file you are creating. Compatibility issues determine whether movie clips (which can be included as interactive material) will play in the result, or not. If compatibility is set to Acrobat 6, they will.

High-res
The only important setting is the page range to include. Otherwise, these settings will not affect the creation of a high-res PDF.

Compression

Compression settings are particularly important as they determine how the images will be handled.

At the foot of the settings area are two checkboxes: 'Compress text and line art' and 'Crop image data to frames'. Both are checked as a default, and should remain so as they help to reduce PDF file size without any loss of quality. Text and line art compression is non-lossy, and any part of an image outside the frame in which it has been placed will not display – so it might as well be cropped out.

The main area of this section holds the settings for greyscale, colour and monochrome images. There are two resolution fields for each of those three types. The default 'Pixels per inch' numbers indicate that, for example, greyscale images will be allowed to remain unchanged if they are present at a dpi of 450 or less, but that anything with a greater resolution will be downsampled (i.e. the content of each pixel will be redefined) to the lower resolution of 300dpi. The method set for this downsampling is Bicubic, which creates a larger but a higher-quality result than the alternative Average Downsampling option.

Clearly, any image that has been placed in an InDesign document and then reduced in size will have a higher relative pixel count and will therefore create a larger PDF – and if the requirement is for a small file size, this is counter-productive right up to the downsampling threshold of 450dpi. So, why not just set both numbers to 300?

Downsampling Test
The images on the next page (fig. **12.4**) are made up of eight duplicate images arranged in four pairs of two. The left-hand image in each pair was generated in test 1, and the right-hand image in test 2. The first pair were both 300dpi, the second 425dpi, the third 450dpi and the fourth 475dpi.

The PDF/X1a:2001 preset was used for both tests. In test 1 the settings were left unchanged. As these will downsample an image only if it is above 450dpi, the left-hand image in pair 4 (at 475dpi) was the only one to be downsampled to 300dpi. As the dpi of the other three left-hand images was at or below 450 they were left unchanged.

In test 2, the 'Downsample images below' setting was changed to 300. So, the only image not to undergo the

12.4 (Top Row) To see if the downsampling presets made any difference in the resulting files, eight copies of the same image were made, each being subjected to different settings.

12.5 Four copies of the same image, each saved at a different dpi and then placed here at the same size to allow any differences to be seen. Top left: 300; top right: 425; bottom left: 450; bottom right: 475.

downsampling process was the right-hand image in pair 1 – which was already set to 300dpi.

There was a considerable size difference between the two PDF documents: test 1 was 2.7MB, while test 2 was only 2.1MB.

While comparing the images, also bear in mind that each successive pair printed smaller than the original, as the relative dpi increased; they are all shown here, side by side, at the same size purely for ease of comparison. In fact their true printing sizes are described in fig. **12.5**.

Low-res

As the consideration here is to produce a small file size at a reasonable quality, I usually change both fields in the colour and greyscale areas to 96, and both to 300 for monochrome. As this creates a smaller file size than would otherwise be the case, I then turn the image quality from low to medium. If the file size is still smaller than necessary, I might re-run the PDF with the quality set to 'high'.

High-res

When creating the side-by-side images for fig.12.4 I was of course working (in Photoshop) with pixels rather than rasterized dots, and while there were some very slight differences between images that had been downsampled compared to those that had not, I doubt very much if they are the kind of differences that will ever be noticed. Therefore, I see no reason – especially when you also consider the difference in the resulting file sizes – to leave the pairs of numbers for greyscale, colour and monochrome images in any high-res PDF preset at their default settings. Instead, I change them to 300/300, 300/300 and 1200/1200 respectively (fig. **12.6**).

Below this area for both colour and greyscale images are two fields that deal with what, if any, method of compression will be used to further decrease the file size. I used to feel that the setting of Automatic (JPEG) could not possibly be as good as None, which does not compress the images at all. 'Why', I thought, 'would I want to bring JPEG compression anywhere near my carefully saved TIFF files?' In fact, when Automatic (JPEG) is combined with Maximum in the Image Quality field directly below it, you will not be able to see any difference at all. Your images will look exactly the same as if you had chosen None. The real difference is in the resulting file size: instead of a whopping 6.9MB file, I ended up with 2.1MB.

The default CCITT Group 4 compression for monochrome images is non-lossy and safe to use for RGB and CMYK output.

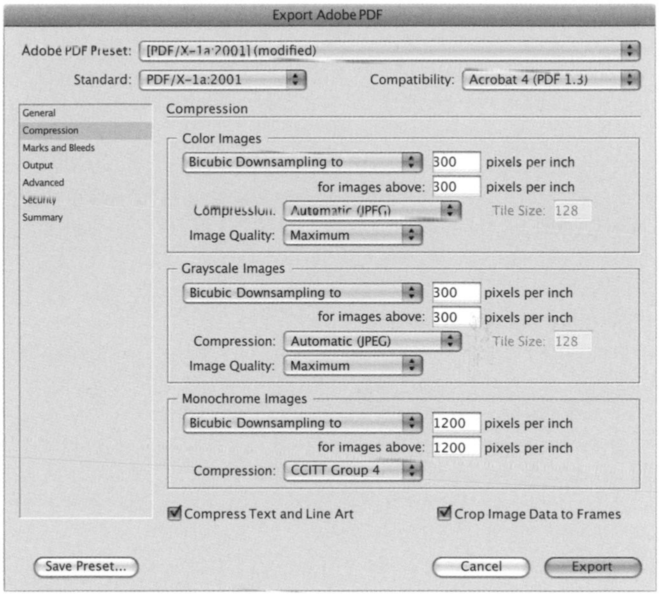

12.6 The Compression settings.

Using Adobe Acrobat

Adobe Acrobat is another area where graphic designers tend to give it their best shot and then sit back in the hope that someone else will take care of any mistakes later. However, this is unlikely to happen. The great benefit to the printer is that a PDF file is complete: it contains all the design elements, all the images, all the fonts; all they have to do is make the plates and print. Only if something fairly extreme crops up are they likely to flag any errors, so it is usually a case of whatever is in there, prints.

With every year that passes, more printers refuse to deal with native InDesign or Quark files and so on, and will only accept files in PDF format because, from their point of view, they are much easier to deal with. By making that decision they no longer have to maintain the knowledge base required to deal with a wide range of incoming work. Instead, all the responsibility for getting the job right is in the hands of the graphic designer. All the printer has to do is receive the PDF file, and print it – mistakes and all.

From the designer's point of view, PDF files are generally uneditable. Certain things can sometimes be changed, but usually you are much better off going back to the native file, fixing the error, and creating a new PDF. However, details such as trapping, image calibration, and – perhaps the biggest problem of all – tagging the whole thing with the correct CMS – all need to be taken care of beforehand, by the designer.

The good news is that creating a good PDF is not that difficult, especially if you use the Export option and know how to adjust the Adobe Acrobat presets to your advantage.

With Adobe Acrobat you can create anything from a low-resolution RGB file suitable for on-screen viewing (which can include a variety of interactive objects) to a high-resolution file containing all the fonts and CMYK images that is ready to print. This can include bleeds, slug areas, crop marks, printer's marks, everything – even Pantone colours.

Until recently there were two options available when creating a PDF: Acrobat Distiller and Acrobat PDF Writer. Both allowed the creation of an accurate image of the finished art in a format that could be readily understood by both PCs and Macs, which could then be printed to plates by imagesetters. Both methods were more difficult than today's option: File > Export.

12.7 The X1a preset.

It is possible that an EPS image will prevent the successful creation of a PDF file on your system. If that happens, you will need to either recreate it, perhaps as a TIFF or PSD file, or leave it out. If it will not print on your PostScript printer (in this case, Acrobat), then it will not print on your printer's imagesetter, either.

If you are using InDesign or QuarkXPress, you are in luck. InDesign can interface with Acrobat, another Adobe product, better than just about anything else. But both programs allow you to choose File > Export > Adobe PDF as the output option.

There are plenty of books available that will take you through every PDF option, so I am going to concentrate on the ones that are particularly important for graphic designers wishing to output either high-res files for print, or lower-resolution files for website, emailing, and/or the inclusion of interactive elements.

You will need to have a PostScript printer already installed on your system – Mac or PC – before you can use Acrobat to create a PDF file.

PDF Presets

If a PDF document is intended to be sent as an email attachment or placed on a website, use the Smallest File Size preset. If you are sending it out for commercial printing, either use Press Quality or, slightly better, but a little more involved, PDF/X1a:2001. All of these can be edited, and the result saved under a new name for future use (fig. **12.7**).

In InDesign, the benefit of using the Smallest File Size preset is that everything in it already points towards the creation of a small RGB file. The advantages of the PDF/X1a preset are that you can specify the CMYK colour-management settings governing the output of the PDF file without actually embedding the profiles themselves; you can also set the level of the **Transparency Flattener** preset.

 NB   If you are trying to create a PDF from a file that contains spot colours in the form of DCS2 or PSD files, read the end of 'Typical scenario 3' in Chapter 10. Normal CMYK and greyscale EPS files, however, should not need any special treatment.

Marks
and Bleeds

Low-res

When making a low-res PDF I do not check the box marked 'All printer's marks', as doing so invariably results in questions from the client. 'What are all those little squares of colour?' or 'There are funny little lines near the corners!' To avoid these, it is usually better – whether making a file for the client, or to put on a website – to create a PDF of the final page area and nothing more. Therefore, bleeds and slug areas are also not normally included.

High-res

When making a high-res PDF for print, I always check the 'All printer's marks' box. Then, everything useful to the printer is included, especially the colour bars. The printer can read the density of the pure CMYK tints in these (as well as a variety of other combinations) on the proof, and compare them to the density of the same colour boxes on the sheets coming off the press.

The one thing I usually change here is the Offset value. The three fields in this area refer to the trim and bleed marks, those 'funny little lines near the corners'. The inner set tell the printer the final trim of the page, while those just beyond them indicate the bleed area. An offset of 2.117mm, the default, puts the end of the trims inside the bleed area of 3mm, so I usually increase it to this amount so that nothing impinges on the live area (fig. **12.8**).

Bleed and Slug

To include these, check the 'Use document bleed settings' box. It will then pick up whatever bleeds have been specified in the document. Alternatively, you can enter other dimensions in the fields below.

The slug area, an additional area greater than the page (and bleed) that you can specify as part of a) your InDesign document and b) the resulting PDF, can be used to hold information such as the position of folds. For instance, in a tri-fold brochure (which actually has two and *not* three folds) is made up of three panels: a front cover, a back cover and a fold-in panel. The fold-in panel clearly has to be slightly narrower than the others in order to fold inside without being scrunched. And that's where graphic designers and printers part company. Designers usually assume that the other two panels, front and back cover, should be the same – whereas printers know that unless the front cover is very slightly wider than the back cover, it is difficult to open. Allow a very slight overlap, however, and it is easy. All three panels are

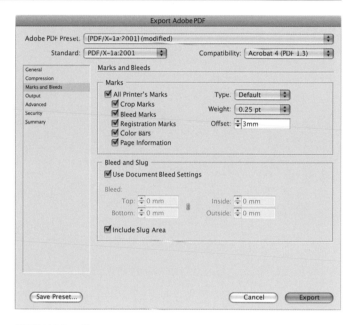

12.8 The Marks settings.

slightly different widths, so the position of the folds is crucial to a successful brochure. These can be specified using dotted lines (not solid, or the printer might cut along them) placed in a 10mm slug, which therefore extends 7mm outside the bleed area.

To ensure the slug is included in the PDF, check the 'Include slug area' box (see fig. 12.8).

12.9 Destination options under Output.

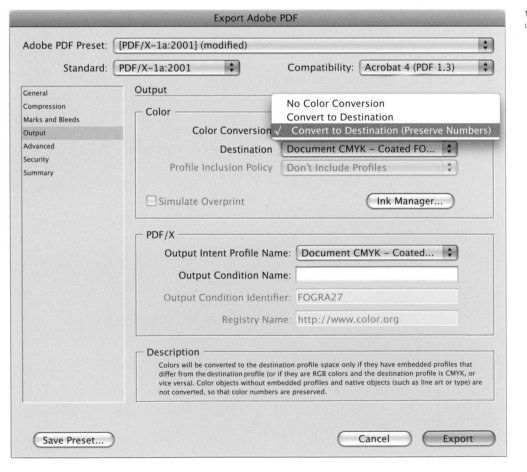

12.10 Colour conversion options under Output.

Output

The Output section determines how the various elements of your document are tagged, or not. Specifying the correct Colour Conversion and Destination Profile will lead not only to a more successful appearance on computer screens but particularly for output on a press, when they are vitally important.

Low-res

The default CMS applies a destination profile, usually beginning with the letters 'sRGB', which is fine as is and requires no adjustment. Colours will be converted to this profile, and those profiles will then be embedded, thus ensuring that they help to control the PDF document's subsequent appearance.

High-res

For a general discussion of CMS, see page 72.

Imagine an example where a document will be printed on a sheet-fed offset press with a dot gain of 10%, but the output profile instead adjusts for a 20% gain.

Normal sheet-fed presses generate roughly 10% dot gain, meaning that a 50% dot in the digital file will print closer to a value of 60%, leading to dark and muddy mid-tones.

The correct profile would adjust the value of the in-coming dot, lightening it to roughly 40% (but without changing how it appears on screen in Photoshop). The printing process then adds 10% dot gain, and the final output is back where it should be at 50%.

However, if the default Photoshop etc. settings are left in place, which are appropriate to printing on a web but *not* a sheet-fed press, dot gain is approximately double the sheet-fed values.

So: the job, destined for a sheet-fed press, has the mid-tones artificially decreased from 50% to 30%. But, the sheet-fed process only brings them back up to 40% – so the mid-tones end up looking washed out.

That is why profiles are so important. If you are in any doubt as to the correct profile to put in place, talk to your printer.

As most printing work takes place on sheet-fed rather than web presses, the profile of Europe Prepress 3 should be set in place. Do this in Bridge, as it will synchronize profiles across all the relevant software in the CS suite. Open Bridge, choose Edit > Creative Suite Colour Settings, and then click on 'Show expanded list of colour settings files'. Select Europe Prepress 3, and click Apply. Do this regardless of whether you live in the UK, Europe *or* the US, as sheet-fed characteristics are very similar in all of these areas.

NB If you choose North America General Purpose 2, or North America Prepress 2, the profile put into place will be for web presses, and *not* sheet-fed, potentially leading to the problem detailed above. If you do choose this, but are printing on a sheet-fed press, you can still set the sheet-fed option as the CMYK profile used in Photoshop. However, the profile for colour created in InDesign etc. cannot be changed in this way and will still output with a profile designed for web presses.

Choosing the Europe Prepress 3 setting puts FOGRA39 into place as the specific CMYK profile, which is an excellent profile for printing onto coated stock. If you are printing onto uncoated stock, it can be changed in Photoshop to FOGRA29. To do this, open Photoshop, choose Edit > Colour Settings, click on the CMYK drop-down list, and choose Uncoated FOGRA29. Doing this will cause your suite-wide settings to be regarded as 'unsynchronized' in Bridge, but they will nevertheless look better in print!

When you know what should be in place and have assigned it in Bridge and/or Photoshop, it should either appear in the Destination field in the Output section of the PDF preset Export window (fig. **12.9**) or (if changed to FOGRA29, for example) chosen from the drop-down list. The same name should also appear in the 'Output intent profile name' area, below. 'Colour conversion' should read 'Convert to destination (preserve numbers)' (fig. **12.10**).

If your work includes Pantone colours, there is no need to do anything else to this window. However, if the included Pantones need to be converted to process colours (which should really be done beforehand to avoid the likelihood of a poor conversion), click on the Ink Manager button and then on 'All spots to process'.

Advanced

Low- and High-res

This section details how fonts will be embedded. The default ('Subset fonts... less than 100%') means that *all* the characters used in *all* the fonts used will be embedded in the resulting PDF (fig. **12.11**). This can be done without infringing on the font licensing you agreed to when buying it, as fonts cannot be extracted from a PDF document.

High-res only

When using PDF/X1a, check there is a Transparency Flattener setting. This determines how any transparency effects or overlaps are translated. Generally, low-res converts them into vector information, which is efficient in terms of file size but may not print so well. High Resolution, the default setting for PDF/X1a (fig. 12.11), generally means that transparency is converted to pixels. Larger files, but better quality. This option cannot be changed in the Smallest File Size preset.

Security

PDF documents can be secured so that they can be read, but not printed; edited, or not; opened, or not. Each depends on a password, which you assign here. This may be needed in order to restrict the distribution of a low-res PDF but is rarely required for high-res.

Summary

This area details the settings you have just put in place and allows you to save it as a report.

At this stage, when all the settings are in place, you can save everything as a custom preset. Click on Save Preset in the lower left corner of the window, and enter a name.

12.11 Advanced PDF options governing embedded fonts.

Using QuarkXPress

Quark is still slightly behind InDesign in that you cannot embed a CMS profile in your PDF. So, you need to have everything figured out beforehand.

Prior to exporting a file as a PDF, choose Utilities > Usage. Check that the fonts showing are the ones you actually used and that the images are all linked correctly. If not, the resulting PDF might be in trouble. If a picture is listed as 'missing', it means Quark cannot find it in the location from which it was originally linked. You will need to update the connection using the Update button. If a font appears that you did not expect, click on Show First to find out where it first appears.

It is not uncommon for Quark and InDesign files to include line spaces that are specified in a default font such as Arial. Since Arial is a resident font on both PC and Mac systems, there is no need to worry. However, if actual text appears in Arial, and it was supposed to be something else, change it to the correct font and resave the file before continuing.

To create a PDF you can now choose File > Export > Layout as PDF. This is much easier than the options available under File > Print, which required the adjustment of many different settings in many different windows.

Creating a low-resolution PDF

After checking that everything is linked correctly, and that there are no missing elements in your document (File > Flight Check), choose File > Export > Layout as PDF. In the Export PDFs window, assign a name and location for the saved file, then either choose an existing preset with no additional editing by making a selection from the Captured Settings list (probably not a great choice, as they all require some kind of adjustment), or click the Options button to open the PDF Export Options window (fig. **12.12**).

Here, you can either choose from the PDF styles listed (fig. **12.13**) under the PDF Style field – all of which can be edited to suit current output requirements – or build an entirely new style

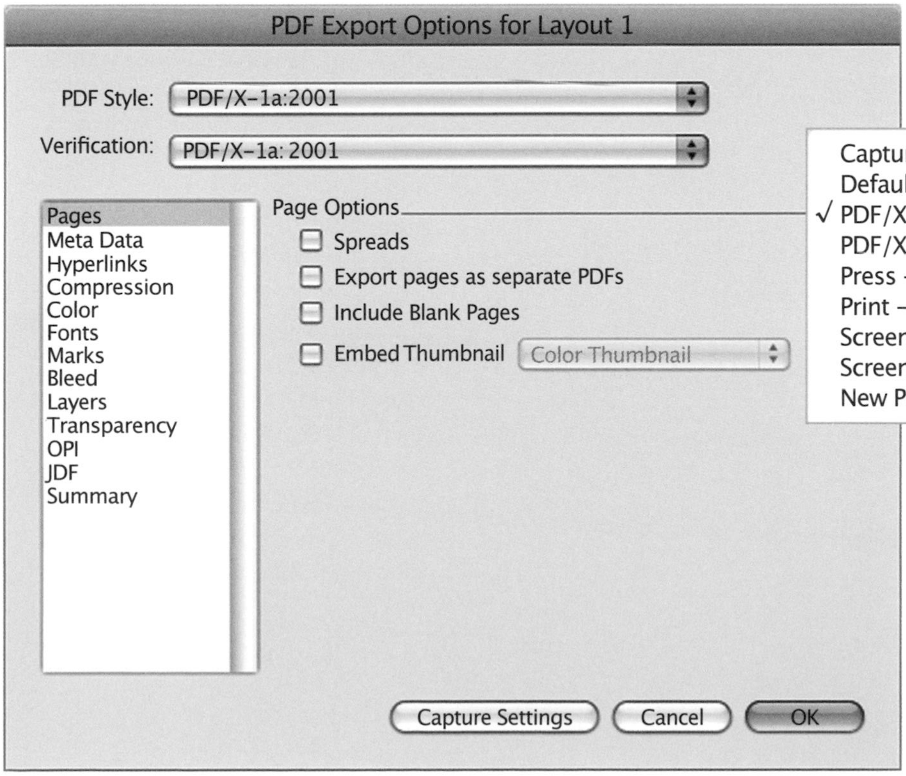

12.12 The Quark PDF Export Options window.
12.13 (Inset) The default PDF presets.

PDF Export Options for Layout 1

PDF Style: PDF/X–1a:2001

Verification: PDF/X–1a: 2001

Pages
Meta Data
Hyperlinks
Compression
Color
Fonts
Marks
Bleed
Layers
Transparency
OPI
JDF
Summary

Page Options
☐ Spreads
☐ Export pages as separate PDFs
☐ Include Blank Pages
☐ Embed Thumbnail Color Thumbnail

Captured Settings
Default PDF Output Style
✓ PDF/X–1a:2001
PDF/X–3:2002
Press – High Quality/High Resolution
Print – Medium Quality/Medium Resolution
Screen – Low Quality/Low Resolution
Screen – Medium Quality/Low Resolution
New PDF Output Style...

Capture Settings   Cancel   OK

by clicking on 'New PDF output style' at the foot of the list. In this case, having named the new style and saved it, it will appear as one of the choices on the drop-down list. You can customize the settings for a new style created in this way in exactly the same manner, and at any time, as you would any other style – see below.

If you are exporting a lower-resolution file either for web use or for sending by email, choose 'Screen – low quality' or 'Screen – medium quality'.

Clicking on the various items in the list on the left-hand side of the Export Options window allows you to change existing values or enter new information, such as in the Meta Data window.

Choose an option under Pages (usually it will be Spreads), then click on Hyperlinks. The default settings ensure that all interactive material – hyperlinks and bookmarks – built into the Quark document will function in the PDF result. You can also choose whether items such as hyperlinks will have a specific, additional visible appearance or appear just as they look on the page. A zoom setting at which the PDF will open can also be set, near the foot of the window.

Compression deals with the display and resolution of all the included images. There are three sections: colour, greyscale and monochrome. The 'Screen – low' settings put 72dpi in place (fig. **12.14**), which is actually the resolution of older Mac screens. The quality of the output can be changed under the Compression settings for all three types of image (fig. **12.15**). However, don't change them for monochrome images, as CCITT Group 4 is a non-lossy form of compression that works very well. Also, make sure the 'Compress text and line art' box is checked, for the same reason.

Colour should generally indicate, regardless of the 'plates' listed below, that the result will be a composite RGB file.

Fonts: if Select All is checked, every character in every font used will be embedded in the PDF result, in a way that does not contravene the licensing you agreed to when they were purchased – which does not usually include the right to send them to the printer.

12.14 Compressions settings for creating a low-resolution PDF.
12.15 Other Compression options.

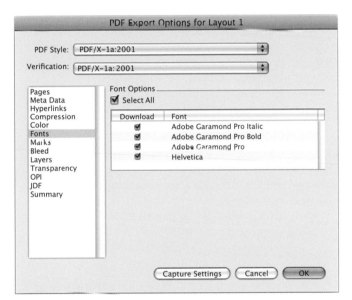

12.16 The Layers options.

12.17 The colour output option for a high-res PDF should usually be Composite CMYK.

12.18 The Font options.

12.19 The Marks options.

12.20 Bleed options.

12.21 Leaving resolution values too low may result in some pixelation. To avoid this, increase them as shown.

Marks refers to registration and trims, and bleed marks can be added if required. The measurements refer to the size of trim marks, and the offset the distance between the end and the edge of the page.

Bleed: if your document contains bleeds, you should specify them here. If you choose Page Items, bleed marks will only be added on pages requiring them. The amount is usually 3mm.

> **NB** Neither marks nor bleeds are usually required in a file created solely for screen viewing. I do not include them in, for example, files sent to clients for their approval, as they usually confuse the client.

Layers: if Select All is checked, all the layers in the file will be included in the PDF result (see fig. **12.16**).

Transparency effects are rendered in various combinations of vector and bitmap. For effects made up of pixels, the resolution can be lower – 72dpi. For vector objects, they require a higher resolution, as they do not mix colours in the same way. If we use a lower resolution for them, visible banding is the likely result.

The last few options are not relevant to the creation of a simple PDF.

High-resolution PDF

If you are making a high-res file for print output, choose 'Press – high quality/high resolution'.

Pages and Meta Data are as mentioned. Hyperlinks will not be available, as they are not part of a print file. In Compression, the default resolution is 300dpi for colour and greyscale images, and 1200dpi for monochrome. Monochrome images require higher resolution as there is no anti-aliasing present to soften them. However, the quality level should be set either to either JPEG High or None, and nothing lower. The same is true for PDF/X-1a, detailed below.

The Colour window shows that in this case the result will be a composite CMYK file rather than RGB (fig. **12.17**).

The Fonts window shows all the fonts used in the document and, as a default, will select and embed all of them (fig. **12.18**).

Marks is as detailed above. However, in the case of a print-ready file, they are essential items to include (fig. **12.19**). Choosing Centred will place registration marks at the centre of each side of the page, just outside the live (i.e. the final, trimmed page size) area.

Bleed should be set to 3mm. You can choose whether to allow bleeds to be marked only on affected pages or throughout the document (fig. **12.20**).

Under Transparency, increase the resolution for drop shadows to 300dpi, and for vector images to 600dpi. This rasterizes them at a higher resolution than the other images. Vectors tend to have sharp edges that may appear pixelated at a lower setting, hence the need to increase the dpi. The Upsample Rotations area is designed to deal with increasing the resolution of rotated images and should be set at 300dpi. If settings are left at 150dpi then it is possible that you will see some pixelation in the end result (fig. **12.21**).

OPI and JDF are more advanced than usually required, and the Summary details everything done in these windows – which you already know, but which may be useful to review.

The settings for PDF/X-1a, another high-res-for-print format, differ in only a few significant ways. Under Colour, only those colours actually used in the document will appear. Under Transparency, the drop shadows should still be increased to a resolution of 300dpi, but the correct resolution for vector rasterization (600dpi) is already in place.

Now that everything is ready to roll, there are some things you should know about printers.

12.22 A guillotine for cutting paper. This machine is capable of cutting right through a stack more than 15cm (6in) thick… but doing so may not be a good idea.

Tools of the Trade, and More

There are a few more things that it is useful to know, as a graphic designer, when taking your job to a print shop.

Film

While most of us will end up using a CTP workflow, some print shops still create film from the digital file. Plates are then made from the film. In this case, the printer owns the film.

Film is technically a tool of the trade, and actually belongs to the printer unless it is specified on the invoice. Then, and only then, is it yours.

If you tell the printers when you call for an estimate that you want to take the film away with you at the end, they might feel inclined to charge you something extra for doing so. On the other hand, if you do not ask for the film until they call you to say that your job is ready to pick up, you might end up paying for the film twice – once for the set they used to print the job (which belongs to them), and once for the set that you want to take away and keep. In fact, there is probably only one set – but you get to pay for it twice.

A way around this, sometimes, is to get a quote for the job, and only after receiving it tell the printer that you want the film to be specified on the invoice. They will be less inclined at that point to tell you that there will an additional charge… so, this method is a bit sneaky.

Incidentally, while it is sometimes worth making sure that the film is yours to walk away with, this is almost never the case with plates. For one thing, you would have to take them to another shop with exactly the same press. Also, it is easy to damage plates and harder to transport them once they have been on a press, as the edges are crimped from the machine grippers. Because of their sensitivity and odd shape, it is almost certain that by the time you have gone to all the trouble to get them on another press, you will find there is a tiny scratch somewhere that nobody noticed before. And scratches, of course, will show up on the print. If they are in a blank area, they can be dealt with. If they are across a halftone, on the other hand, the plate is scrap and it has all been a waste of time for everybody – time that somebody will want to charge you for.

Over- and under-runs

Another unpleasant surprise awaits those who need a very specific number of copies of a job printed: if, for example, you have ordered 1,000 copies of a programme for the 1,000 people attending an event, but the printers hand over only 900.

Despite what you might think, they are probably under no legal obligation to put the job back on the press. Of course, they will make an adjustment to your bill – but that is also likely to be a shock. It will not be 10% less than the estimate, even though they have come up 10% short on delivery. That is because the job is divided into two areas: set-up and production. Set-up costs are things like film, plates and setting up machinery such as folders. All this costs the same whether they run one copy or 100,000. Production costs are things like paper, press time, folding time, etc. Obviously, these will vary according to the quantity involved. In this case, you will not get any reduction on the set-up side of things, but you would get a 10% reduction on the production costs.

However, you cannot ask the printers to put your job back on the press and print the other 100 copies. Trade conventions in the UK and the US allow as much as a 10% over- or under-run, and the only way to avoid it is to a) read the small print if you are signing a contract, or b) make an agreement beforehand with the printers, in writing, that they supply not less than a specific quantity. In the US, the percentage actually varies from state to state, but tends to be lower than in the UK – for example, in California, it is typically 3%. Of course, in order to guarantee delivery of a fixed number of copies, the printers will probably feel the need to order slightly more paper than they otherwise would, which means they also have to allow for slightly more press time, folding time, binding time, etc. So under these circumstances you should expect to pay a little more.

Cutter draw

There is a nasty little phenomenon that you should know about regarding the trimming of your job, because it can affect the quality of the final result even if everything goes well on the press.

It particularly affects cross-overs. These are images that cross over the binding in order to appear on adjacent left- and right-hand pages in a double-page spread. This means each half is printed on a different press sheet. The complete cross-over image appears only when the sheets are collated, folded and trimmed properly.

If cutting (fig. **12.22**) is being done prior to the folding (which is most often the case), there is a good chance that you will get some degree of 'cutter draw' in the result (fig. **12.23**). This is when the blade of the cutter bends as it cuts through a stack of paper – and the thicker the stack, the greater the effect. At the top of the stack, everything is cut along a straight line. The closer you get to the bottom of the stack, the more

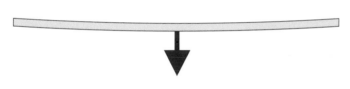

12.23 Seen from the side: the shape of the cutting edge forces the blade into the stack.

Seen from above: as the blade is anchored at both ends, the result of cutter draw is a curved cut.

the blade has curved and the less accurate the registration will be on all the subsequent operations for those sheets. That can mean that your cross-over does not line up properly across the spine.

In order to avoid this, talk to the printers beforehand and make them aware of your concerns. Ask that the bindery staff be told to cut the job in 'small lifts', i.e. a thinner stack of paper as opposed to a thicker one. Again, this will slow things down, so you will be paying a bit more for the job. But remember that old saying: 'You can have it quick, cheap or good. Pick any two'. Printing really is like that.

Sharpening the pencil

Over time, even a really good printer will become slightly complacent about having you as a client, and while in the early days they would trim their quotes wherever possible to give you the most attractive price, they will do so less and less as time goes by. I know this to be a fact, having once been the estimator in a good print shop. So, to keep the price down, you might try the following. Every few jobs, mention that, alas, the boss has asked you to bid this one out to two or three *other* print shops, so would they please keep their pencils sharp when running the numbers as you would prefer to see them get the work.

A final word about printers: when you find some good ones, cherish them. Helpful printers will benefit you and every job you send to them, allowing your clients to recommend you to all their friends with a clear conscience. That is the best kind of publicity you can ever get. I have worked with good printers, and bad, and there is an ocean of difference between them. Most printers will do their absolute best to give you the quality you want, not just because they want you to come back again and again, but because they are decent people who take pride in the job they do.

And a final note about everything else: if this book has helped you, then please use it to help someone else. And I do not mean you have to pass it along to a competitor for free. Just do something for somebody today, and maybe again tomorrow, with this book in mind. Only then will writing it have been worthwhile.

Glossary

Terms that appear in *italics* are explained elsewhere in the glossary.

algorithm
A mathematically generated pattern that determines the level of complexity in the 8 x 8 *pixel* cells comprising a *JPEG* image.

anti-aliased
When a *bitmap* shape (such as text) is anti-aliased it acquires a slight falling-off of tone around the edges. This enables it to blend in visually with another image much more than would otherwise be possible.

artifacting
When a *JPEG algorithm* is set too low, areas that should appear as flat colour in one part of an 8 x 8 *pixel* cell can be distorted by the detail in another.

bit depth
Image complexity, or depth, is described in terms of bits. A 'bit' of information is a single unit of binary information, which can either be 'on' or 'off'. Therefore a '1 bit deep' image is made up of just two colours.

bitmap
Any image that is made up of *pixels* is technically a bitmap, regardless of the actual format. Therefore, *TIFF*, *JPEG* and *GIF* images are all bitmaps.

calibration
A method that adjusts highlights, shadows and mid-tones to determine the overall appearance of an image when printed by a particular method. It can also refer to adjusting the colour settings on a monitor to produce a more accurate screen image.

clipping path
A *vector* outline that acts as a mask, blocking out any areas of the image that fall outside it.

**CMS
(colour-management system)**
Extensively used in Adobe graphics applications, a CMS can be applied using Bridge, which then 'tags' files to produce consistency from screen to print.

CMYK
Cyan, magenta, yellow and black ('key'): the components of the four-colour process printing method.

cold-set ink
A *web offset* printing ink, typically used for newsprint, that dries very rapidly. This avoids the need for in-line dryers.

colour cast
When a colour image has an overall appearance of too much of a particular colour it is said to have a 'colour cast' of that hue.

colour profile
The individual parts of a *CMS* that deal with specific digital tagging of *RGB*, *CMYK*, *greyscale* and spot colours.

Compugraphic
Part computer, part machine, the Compugraphic was a popular *photo-typesetting* system in the 1970s and 1980s.

computer to plate (CTP)
A printing method that avoids the need for *film* by generating the image directly onto the plate.

creep
In book production, a build-up of paper at the binding edge that results in each successive set of pages being pushed out by the thickness of the sheet.

Cromalin
A type of high-quality colour proof made by fusing extremely thin sheets of *film*, each printed with a toner of the appropriate colour, onto a bright white background.

CRT (cathode ray tube)
A cathode ray tube generates an on-screen image by combining red, green and blue light.

dab test
Testing the accuracy of a *Pantone Matching System* ink mix by spreading a very small amount of it onto a sheet of paper. This is often done right beside the press with the printer's finger.

DCS2 (desktop colour separation 2)
A multi-channel file format that allows *spot colours* such as Pantone mixes to be added to *CMYK* images.

densitometer
A hand-held device that measures the density of the ink on a printed sheet.

direct imaging (DI)
A printing method that avoids not only *film* but *plates*, too. DI electrostatically generates the image on a revolving drum in much the same way as a laser printer. Therefore, each successive page can be different.

dither
Scattering *pixels* of one colour across pixels of another creates the visual appearance of a third colour that is not actually present. This enables *GIF* images, which can hold a maximum of 256 colours, to appear to be much more complex.

dot gain
When a *halftone* image is physically (rather than digitally) transferred from one medium to another, the dots tend to change size. Technically, the change undergone by the 50% dot is called 'dot gain', although the term has come to refer more to changes across the entire tonal range.

dpi
Dots per inch, the dots actually being square *pixels*. This is the accepted measurement defining the resolution of an image made up of pixels.

duotone
A duotone is a two-colour image, usually comprising black and a Pantone colour. If the Pantone colour will be a fifth colour in what would otherwise be a four-colour process run, the image will usually be converted back into *CMYK*. However, it can also be saved with the true Pantone channel in place as an *EPS* or *PSD* file. In Adobe Photoshop, duotones can only be created from a *greyscale* image.

EPS (encapsulated PostScript)
An image format capable of holding both *vector* and *bitmap* information.

film
A transparent acetate sheet coated with an opaque photo-sensitive emulsion on one side.

flexography
A printing method capable of printing on non-absorbent surfaces that uses a moulded rubber sheet as a *plate*.

folding dummy
A folded sample of an intended print job that is typically sent to the printer as part of the designer's proof so that possible misunderstandings in folding, cutting and scoring can be avoided.

frequency-modulated screen
See *stochastic screen*.

galley
Photo-typesetting machines of the 1970s and 1980s imaged their text onto long rolls of photographic paper or *film*. These were known as galleys of type.

**GIF
(graphics interchange format)**
An image made up of a restricted (*indexed*) palette of 256 colours, one of which can be designated as transparent. This makes GIF images ideal for websites, where they can be used for irregular shapes such as logos that can then be 'floated' over coloured backgrounds. GIF images are not suitable for inclusion in a job destined for *offset* printing.

glyph
A specific form of character such as a *swash* or small cap alternative to the regular form.

grain direction
The fibres from which paper is made tend to line up together during the manufacturing process. This is known as the grain direction of the sheet. Paper folds more easily and cleanly with the grain than against it.

gravure
A printing method using etched cells in a rigid *plate* to hold more, or less, of the ink, which then results in a correspondingly darker or lighter printed area.

greyscale
An image made up of 256 shades of grey *pixels* that is then printed using black ink.

gripper edge
The edge of a press sheet that is grabbed by a series of mechanical 'grippers' in order to pull it through the press.

halftone
An image that has been converted into a vertical and horizontal grid of dots of different sizes.

HTML (hypertext markup language)
One of the main codes used for website layouts.

image header
Because it is not possible to see an actual *EPS* file when placed into a page layout, an image header (a low-resolution *TIFF* image) appears instead, showing the position and content of the EPS image.

imagesetter
A machine that digitally images *film* and/or *plates*.

imposition
The layout governing how pages in a multi-page job need to be arranged so that they end up in the correct order.

indexed colour
The colour mode of *GIF* images, which can hold a maximum of 256 colours.

interpolation
Mathematically rather than optically increasing the resolution of an image.

JPEG or **JPG (joint photographic experts group)**
An image format supporting *greyscale*, *RGB* and *CMYK* colour but that uses a *lossy* compression method. However, at high-quality levels, the loss is almost impossible to detect, while the file size is much smaller than the same image saved as a *TIFF*. Nevertheless, JPEGs should not be included in a job destined for *offset* printing.

LAB mode
A wide-gamut file format made up of three channels: 'lightness', 'A' and 'B'.

laser proof
When a job is sent to a print shop, it is usually accompanied by a full, laser-printed copy intended to show where everything is supposed to be on the final print. Its accuracy in terms of colour varies a great deal and should usually only be considered as an approximation of the final print.

letterpress
A printing method relying on the assembly of metal type characters and etched images into a matrix, which can then be inked.

ligature
A single typographical character that combines two or more other characters.

Linotype
Part computer, part machine, the Linotype was a popular *photo-typesetting* system in the 1970s and 1980s.

lossless
An image compression method that does not result in any data or quality loss.

lossy
An image compression method that results in a degree of data, and therefore quality, loss.

lpi (lines per inch)
The standard measurement of *halftone* resolution. It refers to the number of rows of halftone dots there are per inch.

moiré pattern
An interference pattern caused by the dot grids ('screens') of two or more colours in an image being set at incorrect angles. This causes the dots to collide unevenly.

Newton's Rings
Pressure points against the glass of a vacuum platemaker caused by small foreign objects trapped inside. These appear as concentric rings of dark colours.

nodes
Anchor points that determine the shape of a *vector* path.

offset litho
A printing method in which the image on a *plate* is transferred ('offset') to an intermediate roller prior to final transfer to the paper.

optimization
Cutting down on image file size while trying to maintain the quality of its appearance.

Pantone Inc.
The Pantone Corporation produces many aids to designers and printers, such as the Pantone Process Guide (for selecting *CMYK* tints) and the *Pantone Matching System*, which allows a wide range of non-CMYK colours to be accurately mixed by formula.

Pantone Matching System
A range of printing ink colours that can be mixed easily by formula from a set of base colours.

PDF (portable document format)
A form of *PostScript* developed by Adobe that enables a printable document to be generated as anything from a low-resolution screen image to a high-resolution file suitable for *offset* printing. This is the format in which most files are now sent to commercial printers.

perfecting
A printing process that applies the image to both sides of the sheet during the same run through the press.

photo-typesetting
Generating text using photographic means, typically using a hybrid machine (such as *Compugraphic*) that is part mechanical and part digital.

picking
This occurs when the ink is unable to stick to the paper and peels back off onto the rollers of the printing press instead.

pixel
The building blocks of digital images, pixels are small squares of colour. The resolution of an image is determined by how many pixels there are per linear inch. The colour range of the pixels is determined by the *bit* depth of the image.

plate
A sheet of, typically, aluminium or zinc coated with a photo-sensitive emulsion. When developed, either the remaining emulsion or the exposed background attracts ink.

posterize
Restricting an image so that it displays only a specific number of colours.

PostScript
A digital encoding language developed by Adobe.

PostScripting
Generating a digital file in a *PostScript* format, usually in order to overcome problems that can arise when transferring a document from a PC computer to a Mac *imagesetter*.

PSD (Photoshop document)
A file format capable of supporting multiple layers, transparency, *clipping paths*, *spot colours* and more. The most versatile image format, PSD files can be placed into InDesign, Quark and Illustrator.

rasterize
This is the method by which a *bitmap* made up of *pixels* (which are square and have no space between them) is turned into a *halftone* made up of round dots arranged on a horizontal and vertical grid.

registration
When a multi-colour image is printed, it is essential that each colour is laid down in exactly the right place. If not, the result is said to be 'out of register'.

RGB
A colour system comprising combinations of red, green and blue light.

RIP (raster image processing)
The means by which *vector* information, i.e a *PostScript* or *PDF* file, is converted into a printable 'raster' image, i.e. one made up of the dots output by the imaging device.

saddle-stitching
A binding method using metal staples for publications such as magazines that usually contain 64 pages or fewer.

screen density
The number of *halftone* dots to a linear inch determines the screen density of an image.

screenprinting
Printing by forcing ink through a membrane stretched over a frame, on which the image acts as a stencil.

set-off
The unwanted transfer of part of a printed image from one sheet to another. This usually occurs within a stack of freshly printed sheets due to a lack of *offset* spray, or from too much ink, or both.

sheet-fed press
A printing press that uses sheets of paper rather than a continuous roll.

sheetwise format
A print run in which a different set of *plates* is used to print each side of the sheet.

signature
A multi-page section of a book that is printed as a single, larger sheet. This can then be folded and collated with any other signatures prior to binding and a final trim.

spot colour or **special colour**
A specific non-*CMYK* ink colour.

stochastic screen (also frequency-modulated screen)
An image generated using an apparently random spray of extremely small dots of colour, which is therefore incapable of generating a *moiré pattern*, regardless of the number of colours involved.

swashes
Alternative character choices within a given typeface, such as more ornate capitals.

TIFF or **TIF (tagged image file format)**
An uncompressed *bitmap* format that supports a variety of colour modes including *greyscale*, *RGB* and *CMYK*.

tint jump
A sudden jump in tint density caused by a meeting of the individual dots comprising the *halftone* screen.

transparency flattening
Low, medium or high transparency flattening determines how transparency is dealt with between overlapping objects when making a *PDF*. Typically, but not always, 'low' means that transparency is generated using a *vector*, while for 'high' it is usually generated using *bitmap* information. 'Medium' uses a combination of both. The PDF/X1a preset allows users to choose between the three levels.

trapping
The enlargement of a light-coloured area so that it slightly overlaps into an adjacent darker colour, thereby compensating for slight imperfections of *registration* on the press that might otherwise cause a gap between the two.

vector
A mathematically defined outline to which colour and thickness can be assigned. This is the native object format for elements drawn using Adobe Illustrator, CorelDRAW and Macromedia Freehand.

web offset litho
A printing method in which the image is transferred from the *plate* to an intermediate roller prior to being transferred to the paper, and which prints on a continuous roll rather than sheets.

work-and-tumble format
A print run in which the paper is printed on one side, then turned long edge over long edge before being run through the press again.

work-and-turn format
A print run in which the paper is printed on one side, then turned short edge over short edge before being run through the press a second time.

Index

Acknowledgements

Almost everything I have learned about offset printing and graphic design has come through the kindness and patience of many fine and generous people. I would therefore like to take this opportunity to thank the following individuals: Barry Adalian and Barry Viney for being the world's best mentors.

Alan Raingley and Jack Butterworth for taking a chance and giving me my first job in commercial offset printing.

Vin Smith for being himself, and also for being the finest printer I have ever met. Robina Courtin for being in a class all of her own in her pursuit of perfection in all things.

Angus Berry for his ability to make light of absolutely everything.

Ron Mullein and Martin Gallagher for their… unique approach to graphic design.

Phil and Grace Sharples, Ed Cain, Jean Stubenrauch, Mark Taylor, Charles Gropman, Eve Kline, Carla Winkler, Sheila Burns and Mark Kroninger for being the best print team I've ever had the pleasure of working with.

Cindy Frank and John Fremont for letting me design so many of their book covers.

Nick Ribush for being almost as picky as I am.

Peter Bone for his assistance with some of the more esoteric software questions and also for his sense of direction. Or lack of it…

David Arnold, Shumi Begum, Zoe Hind, Praveen Hurnam, Ricardo de Jesus, Kess Jones, Iain Macaskill, David Miller, Sarah Paton, Stephen Rea and Mark Young at Academy Class for all their support, and for being such a great bunch of people to work with.

Photo credits go to Beth Dart (page 128), Andy McKee (pages 14, 18, 23, 116, 151) (with many thanks to Mark Downey and his team at Epic Print in Dorchester), Joe Neves (Studio Z Mendocino, Fort Bragg, California) (pages 11, 13), Ven. Ajahn Amaro (pages 86, 102), and Sarinda Newell (page 61). I would also like to thank Jo Lightfoot at Laurence King Publishing for her faith in this project, and my editor Nell Webb for the good humour and great patience she managed to maintain while wading through endless piles of information about printing and graphic design.

And a huge thank you to Frances Kelly, my agent, for all her support, humour and kind words. Without you, Frances, none of this would ever have happened.

Finally, I would like to thank my family, in general and specifically: my late father for introducing me to the world of typography and printing; my mother for refusing to believe that a leaf changes colour in the dark; my brother for thinking up the 'leaf test' in the first place; my sister for being a fellow graphic designer; and my dear wife Linda for her incredible support through good times and bad, and for suggesting that I write this book in the first place.

Mark Gatter

Publisher's photo credits

Images on pages 63, 91, 124 and 127 from iStockphoto.
Photograph on page 76 © Quattrone, Florence.
Photograph on page 134 © Angelo Hornak, London.